Welcome to your Blissful Coloring book.

You can use various coloring tools like, pencils, dual brush pens, gel pens, markers, etc.
Suggestions below.

These mandala designs are a bit funky and untraditional. I hope you enjoy them and I look forward to reading your comments, reviews, and critique.

I do have a Facebook page if you would like to leave comments there.

https://www.facebook.com/AdultColoringBooksbyRo/

<u>Coloring Tool suggestions with great reviews:</u>
1. These pencils can be bought up to 150 pencils at a time:
http://amzn.to/2hnkrbb
2. These dual brush pen markers have a fine tip and brush tip:
http://amzn.to/2hbLRh1
3. These gel pens come in a 200 pack variety:
http://amzn.to/2heYlzi

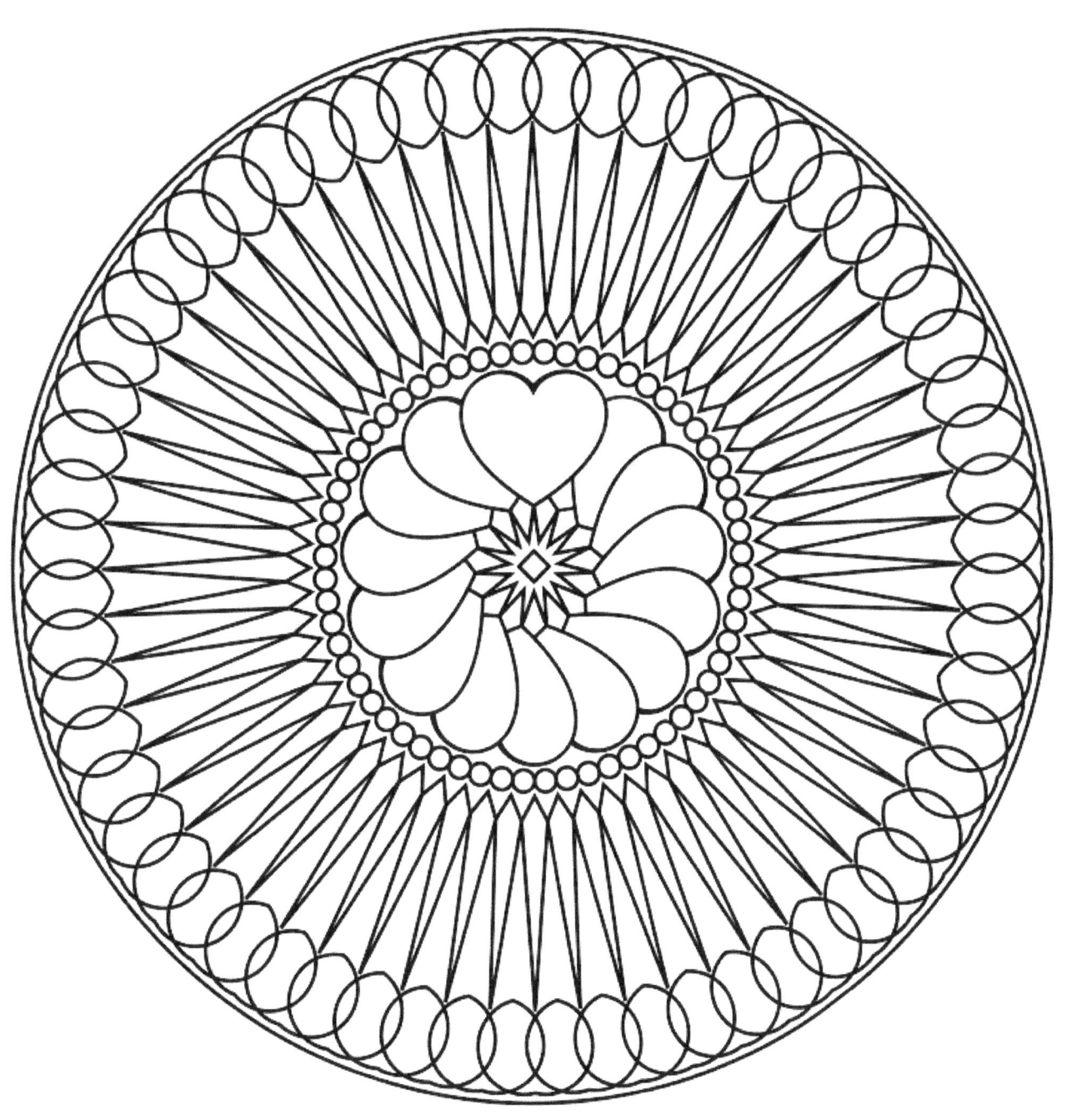

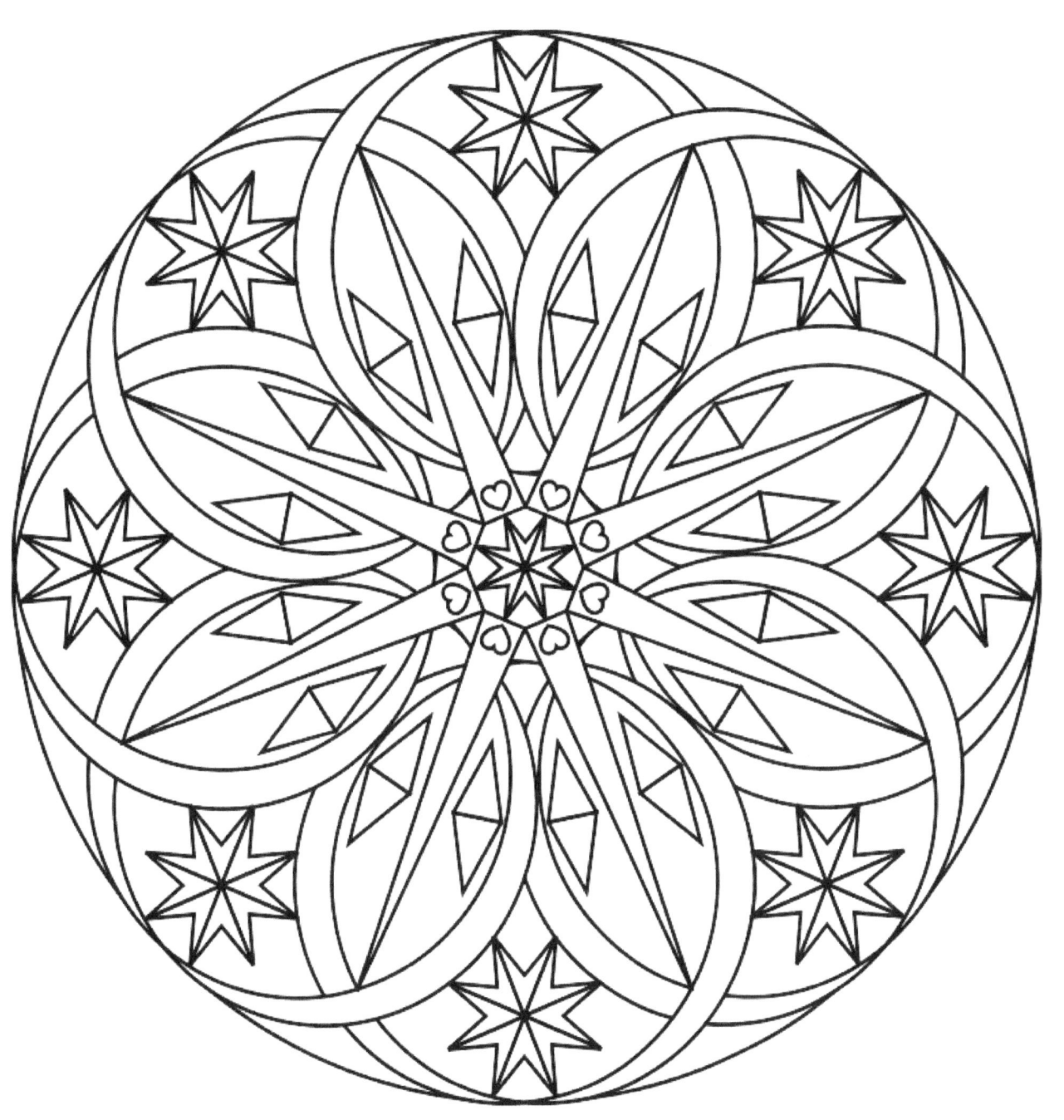

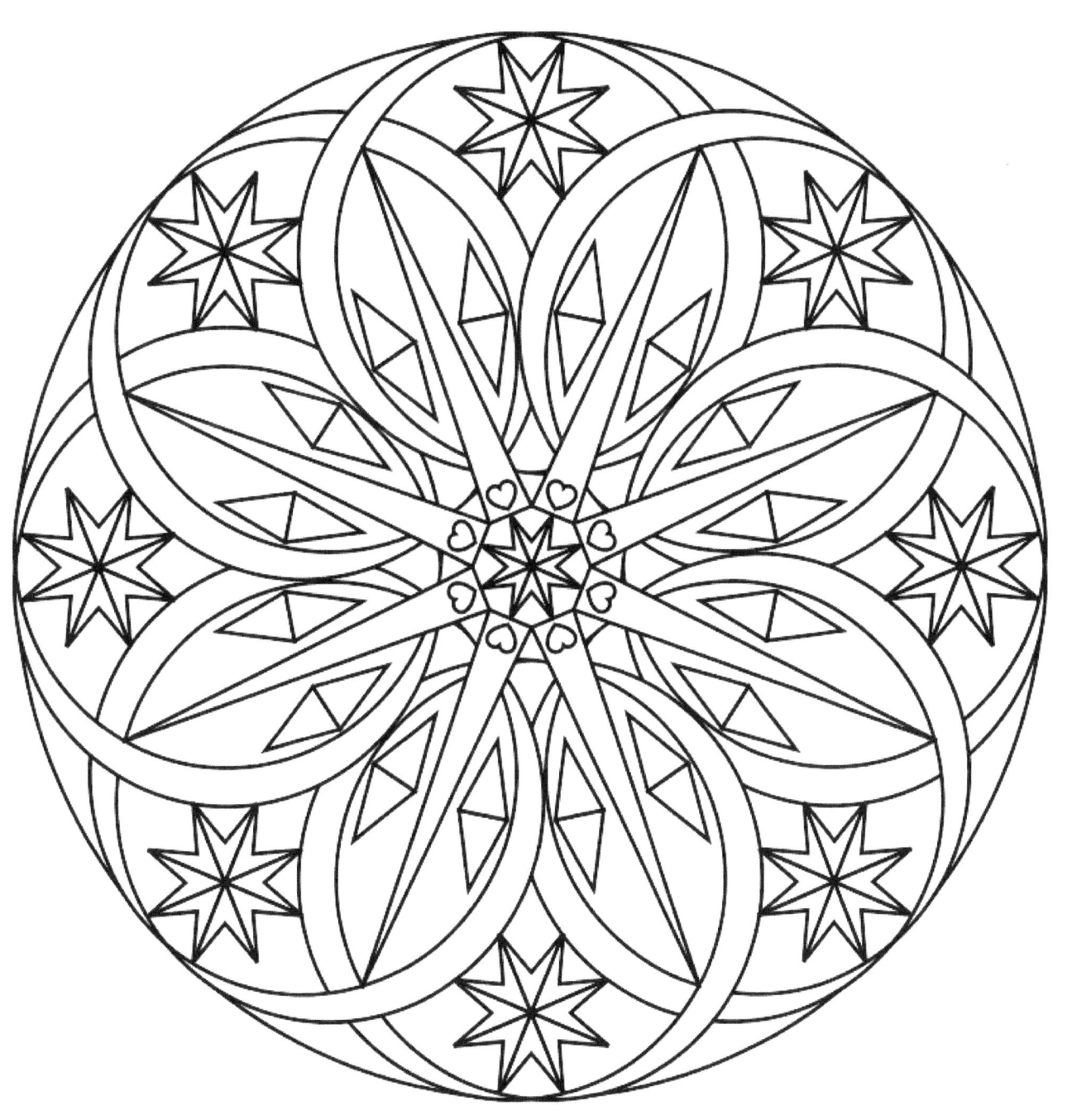

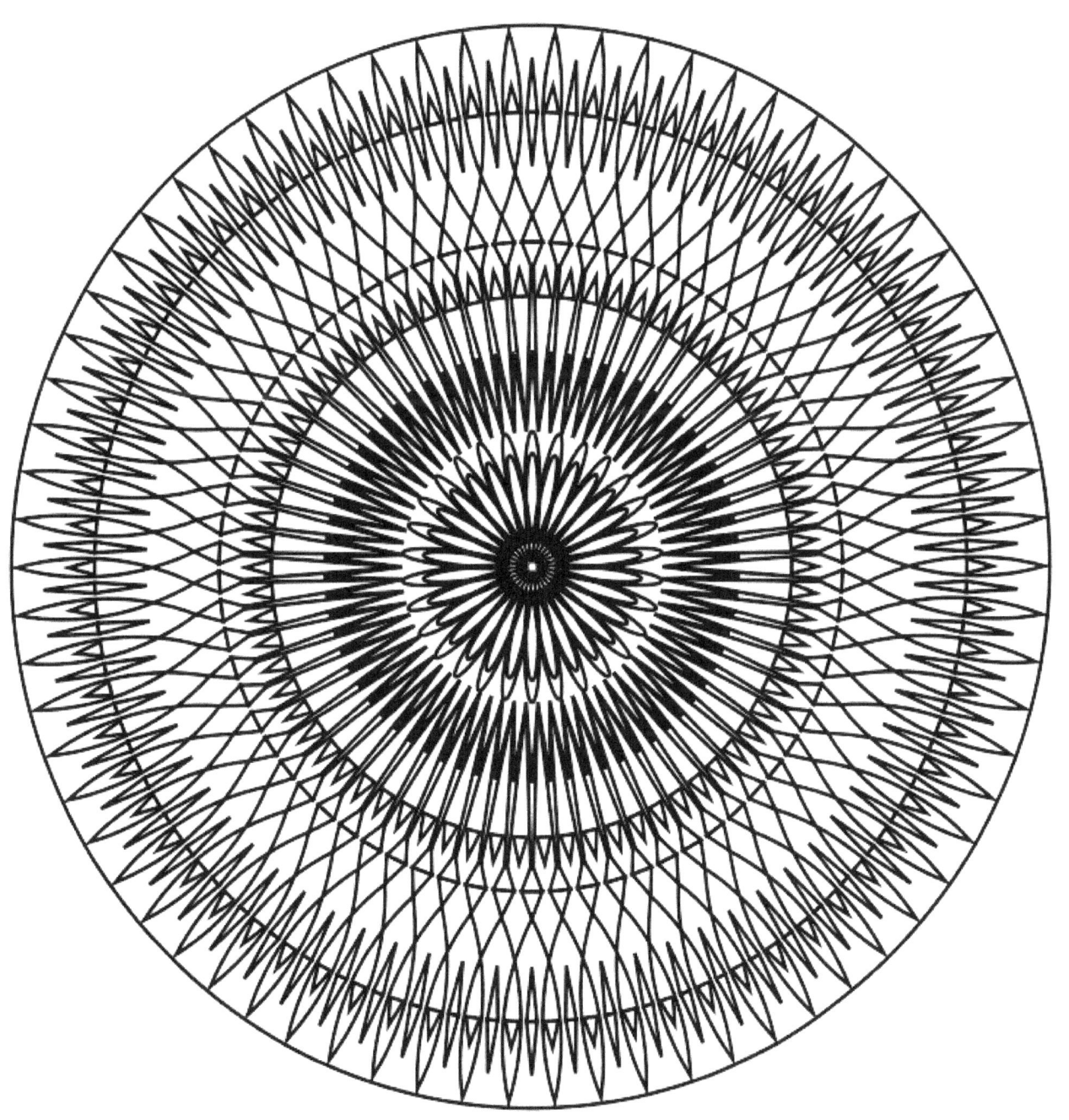

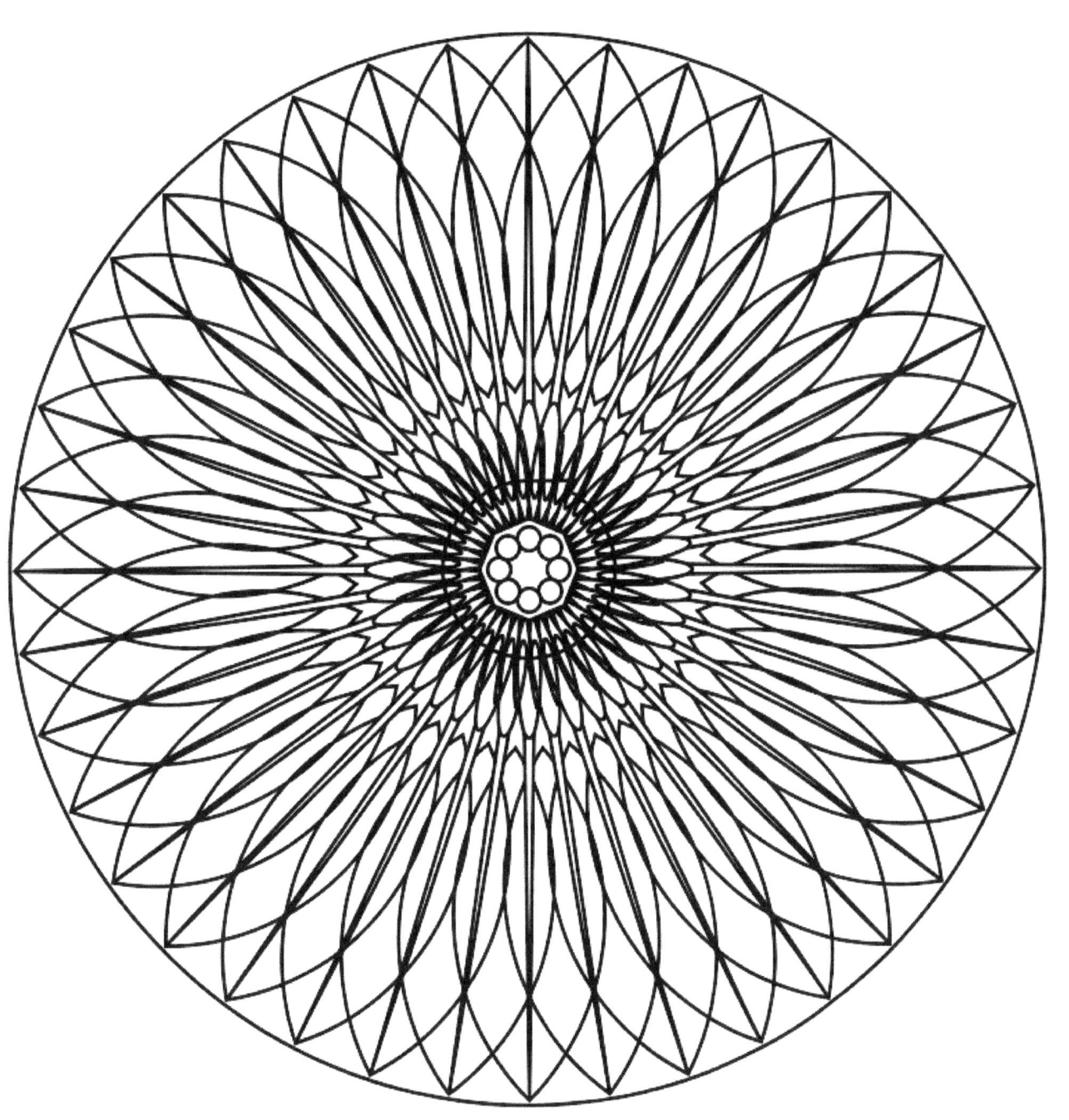

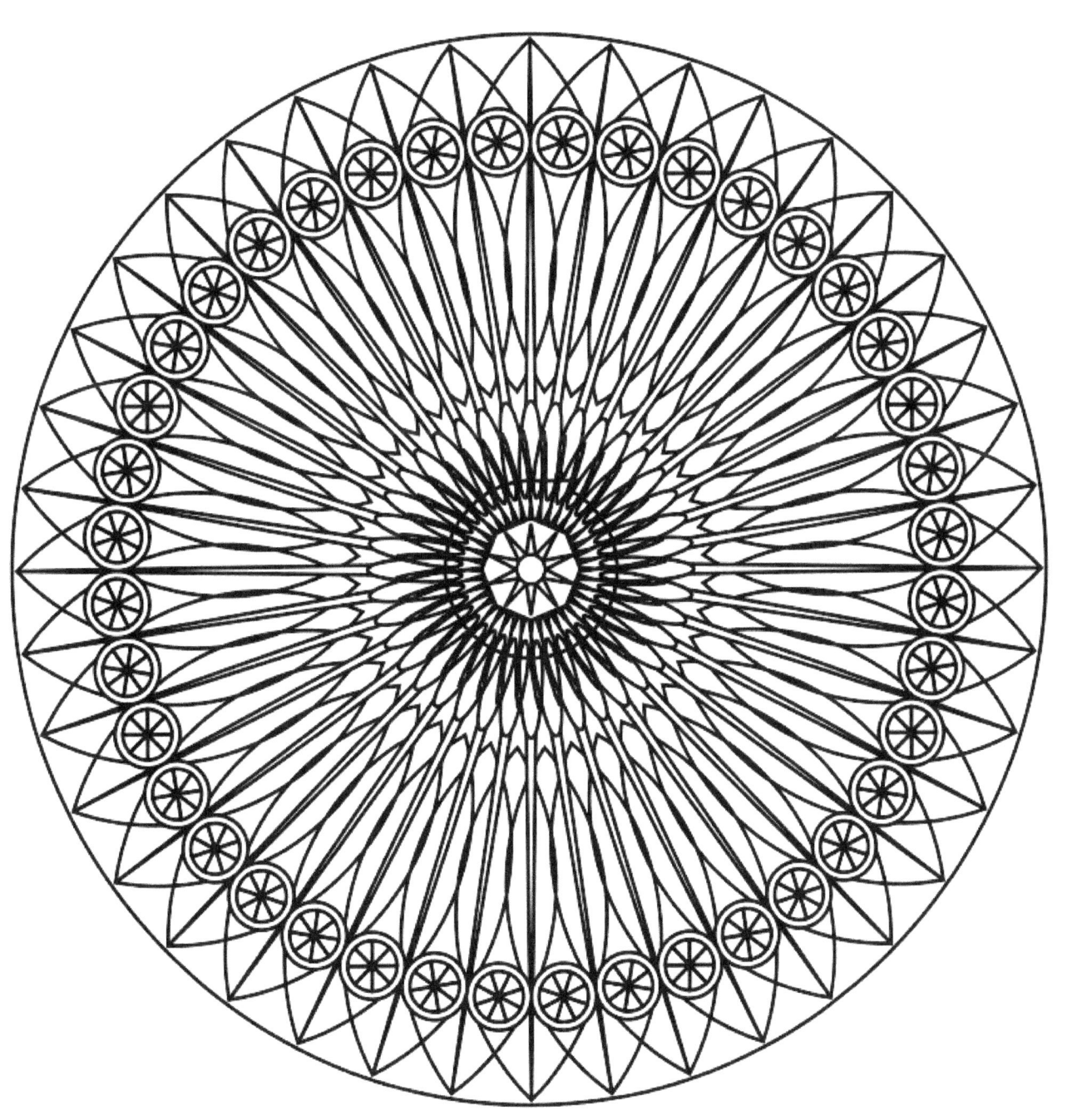

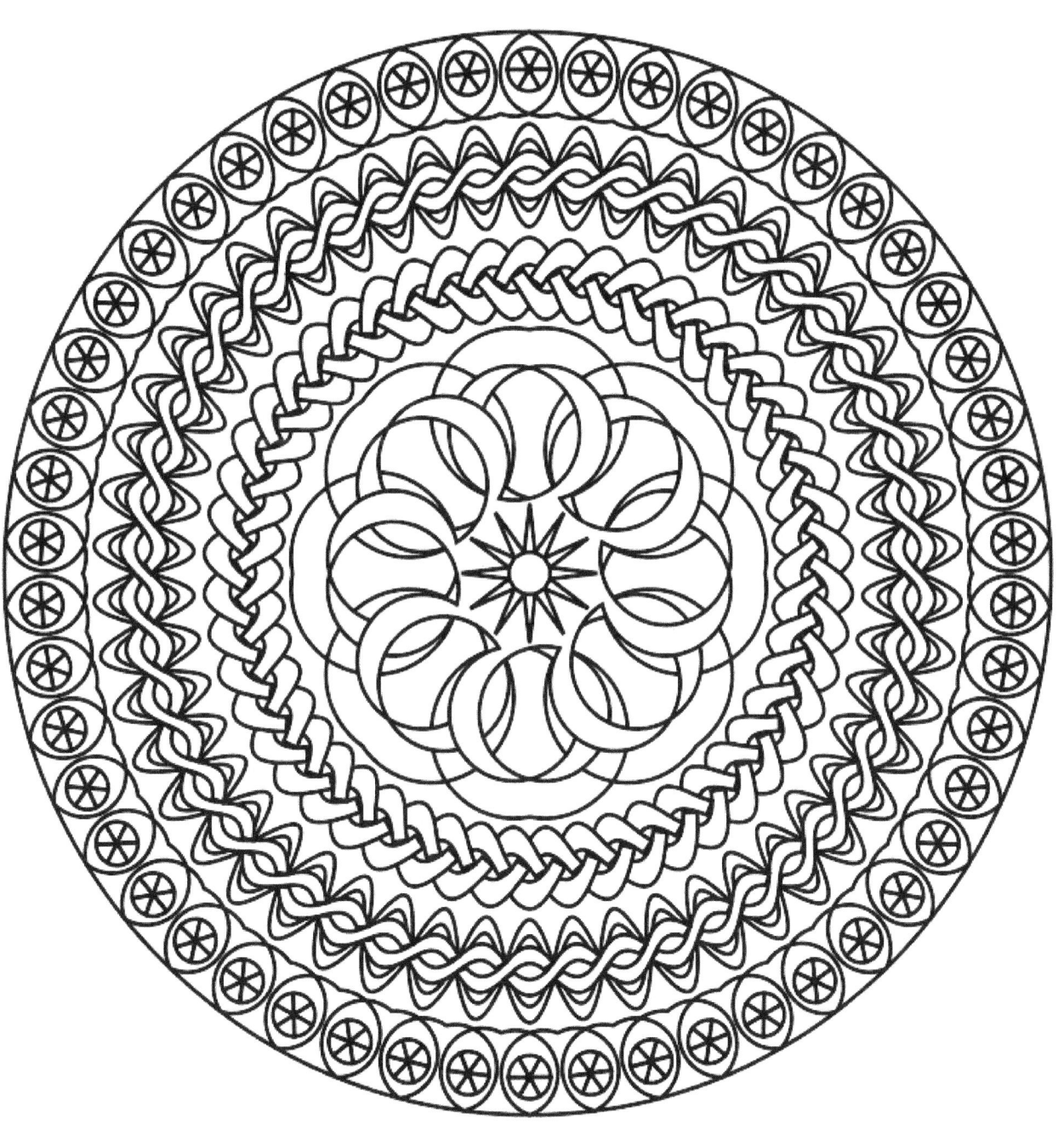

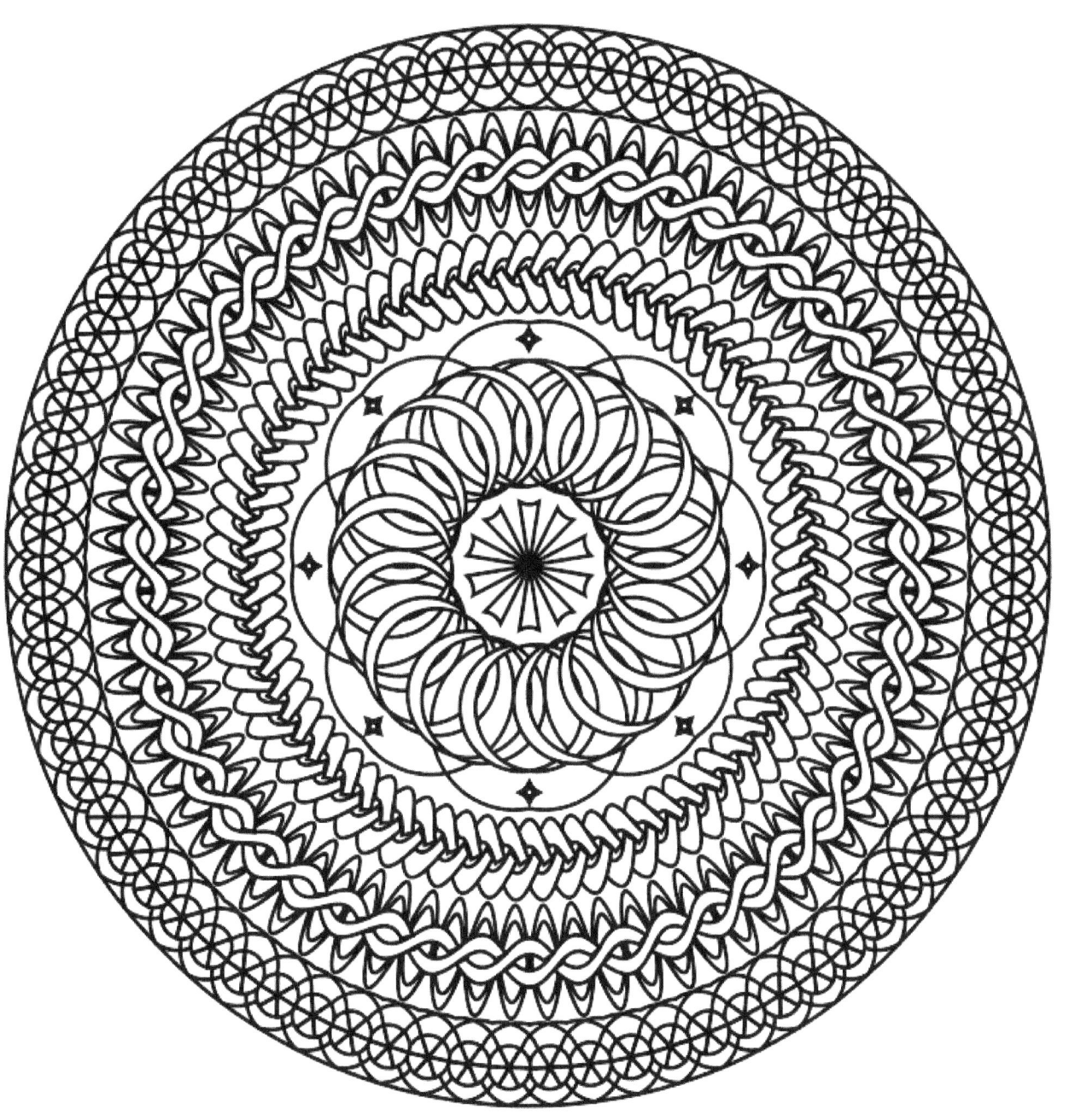

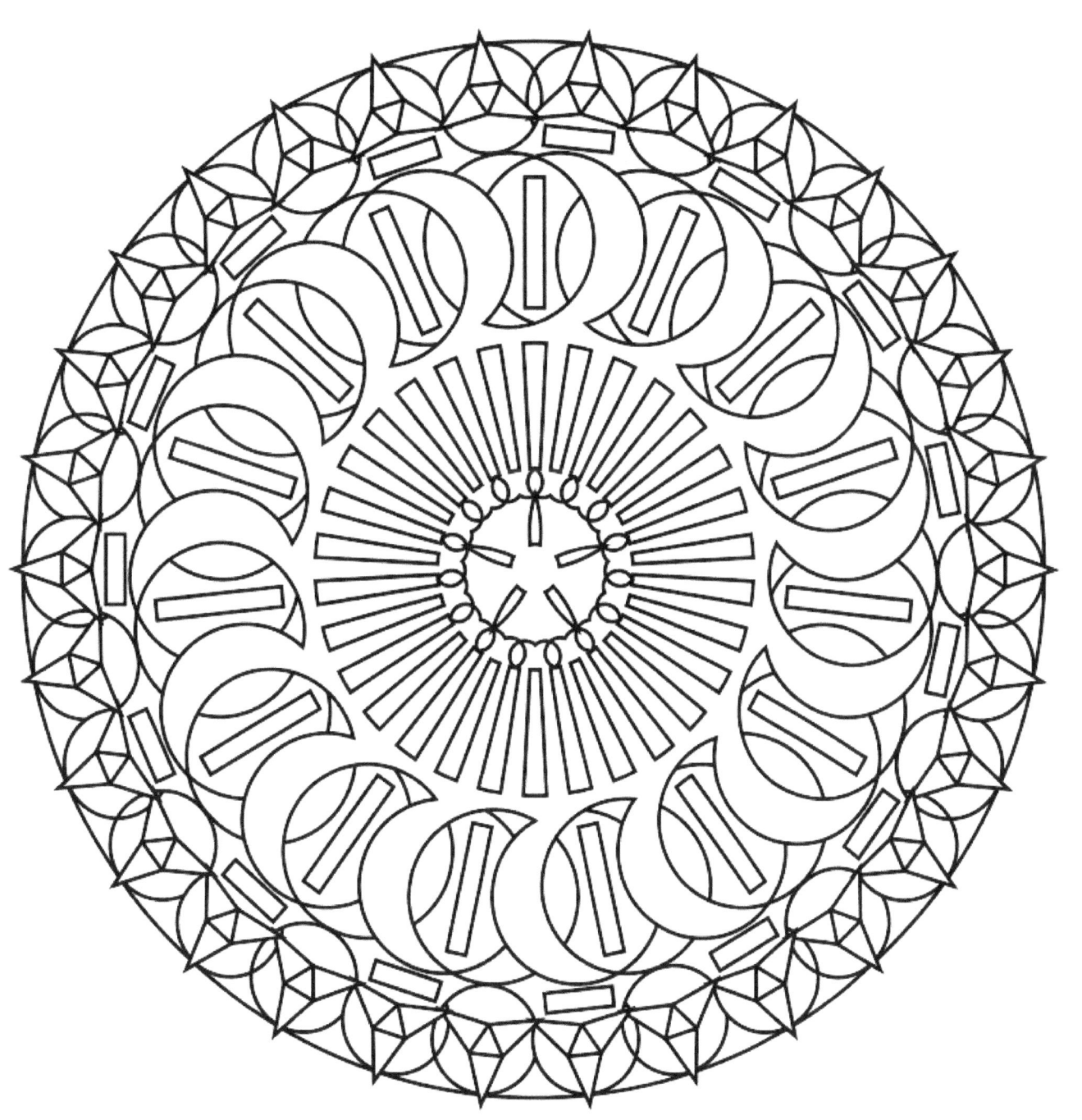

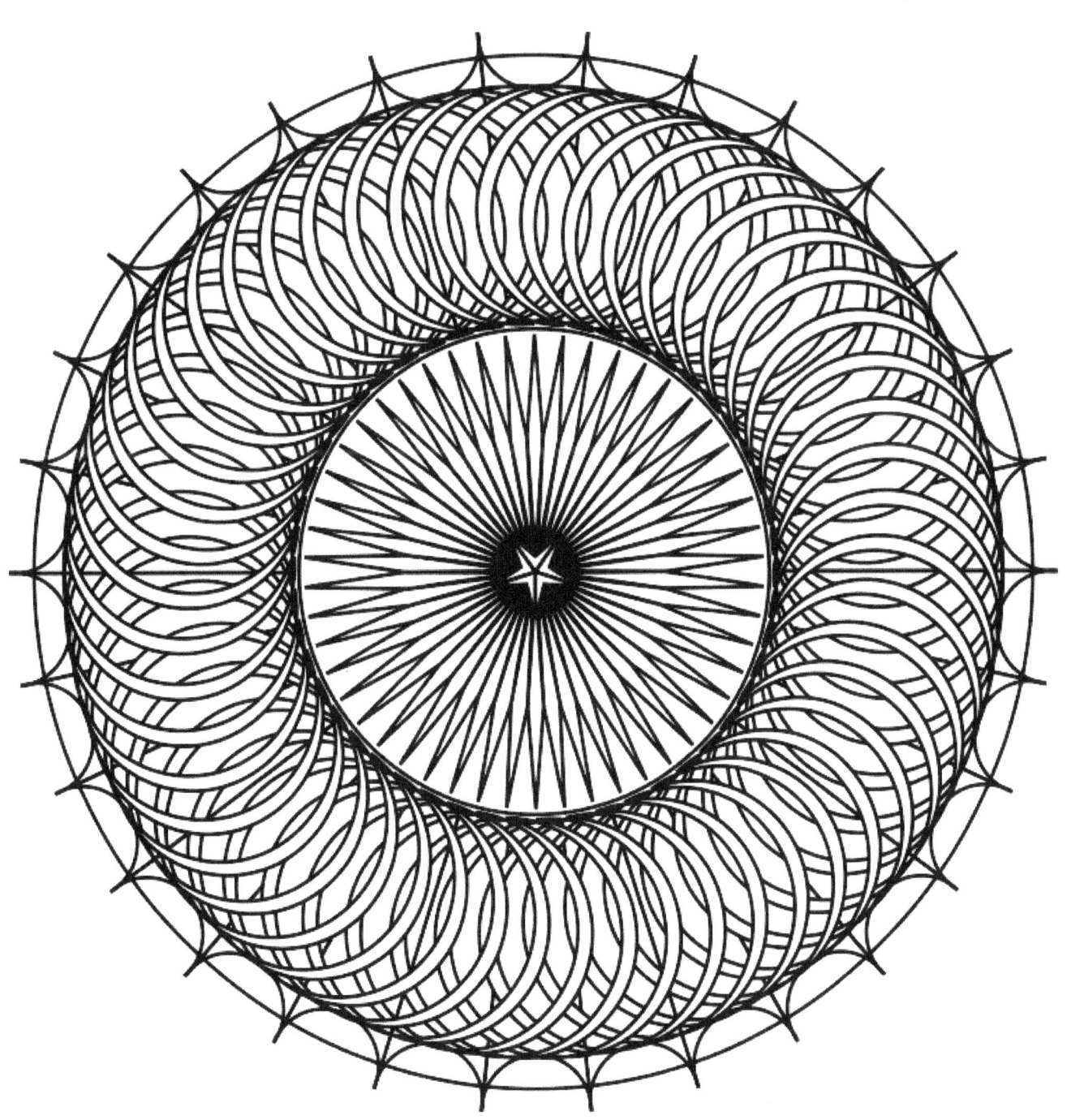

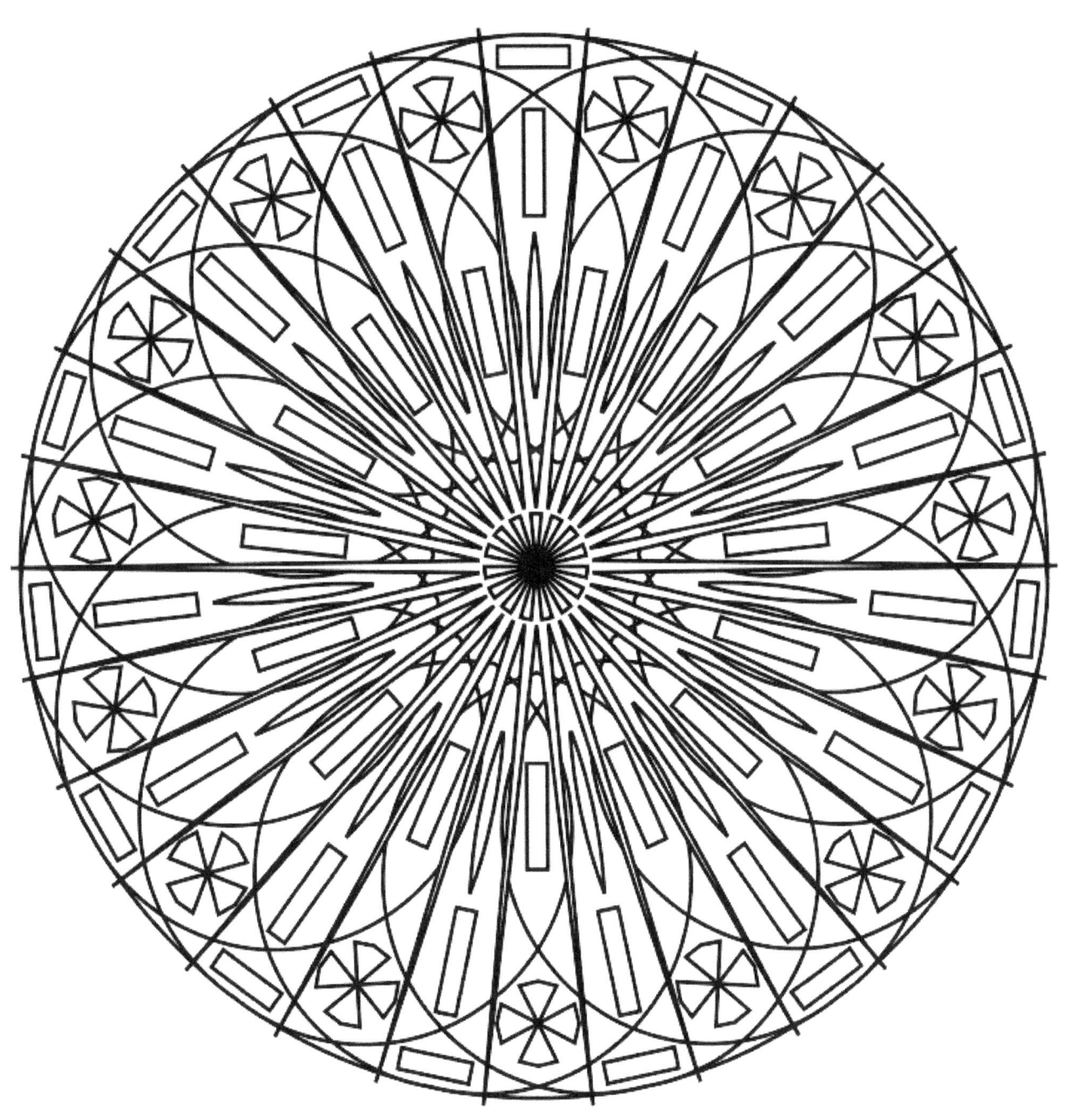

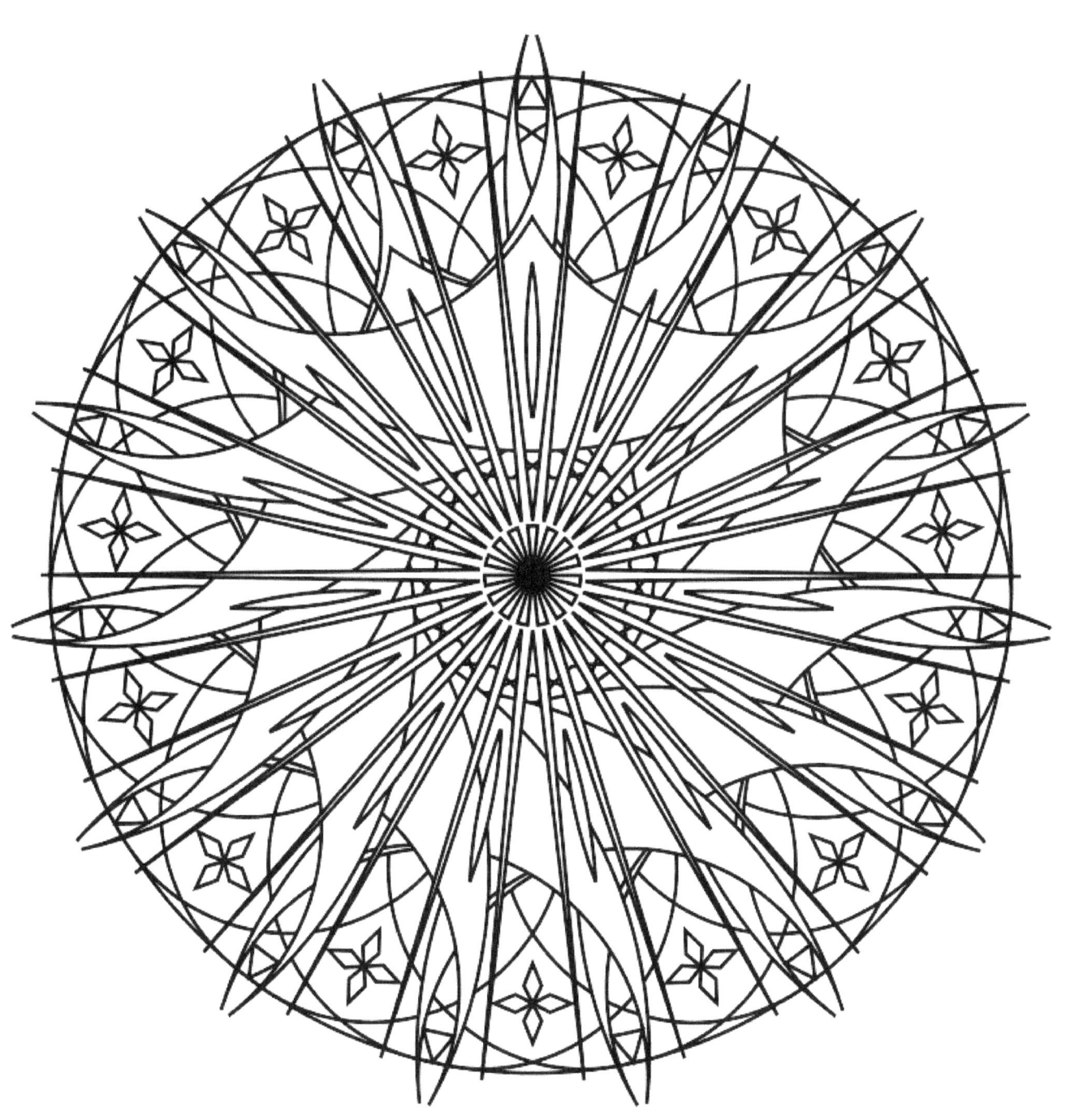

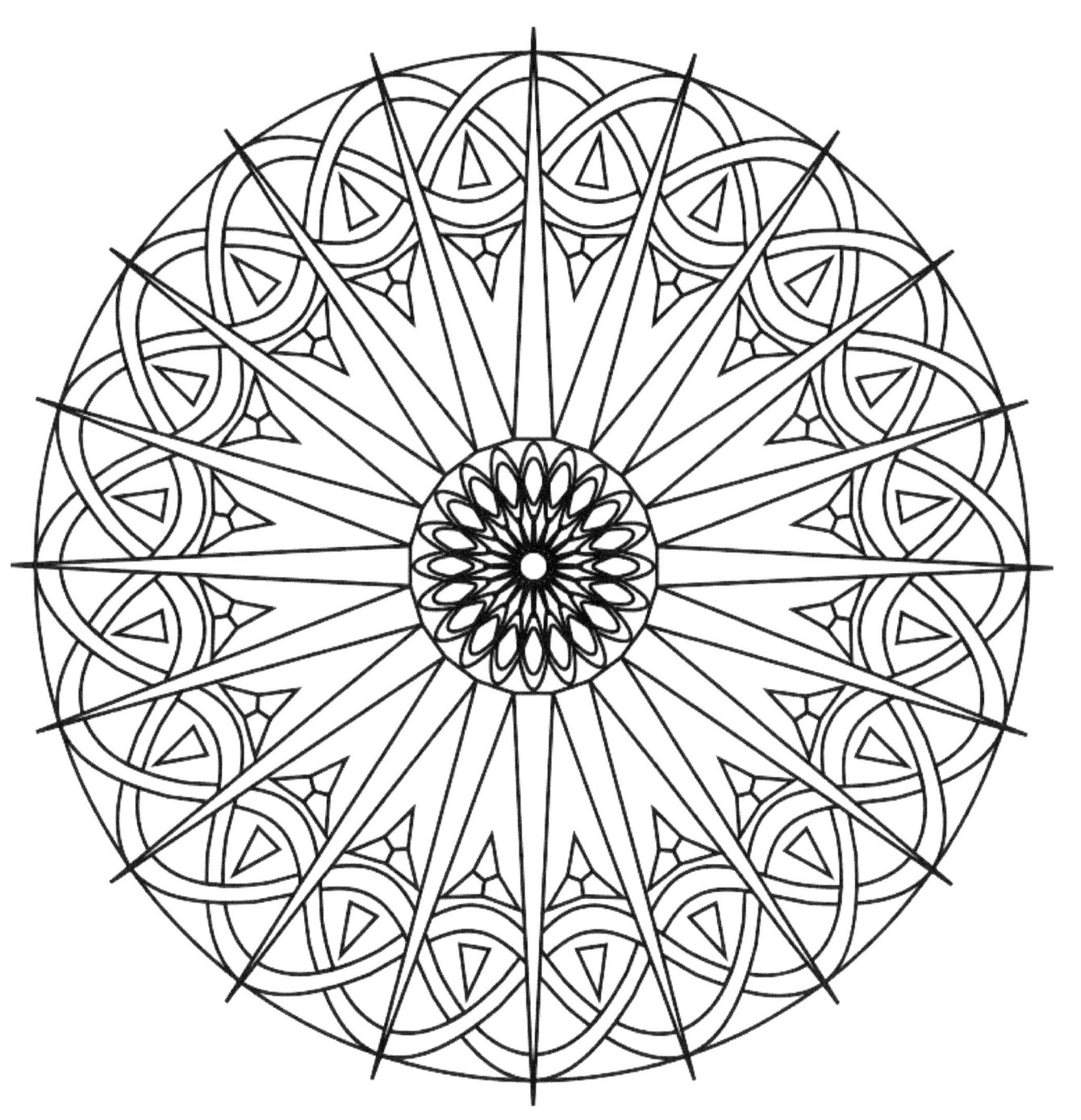

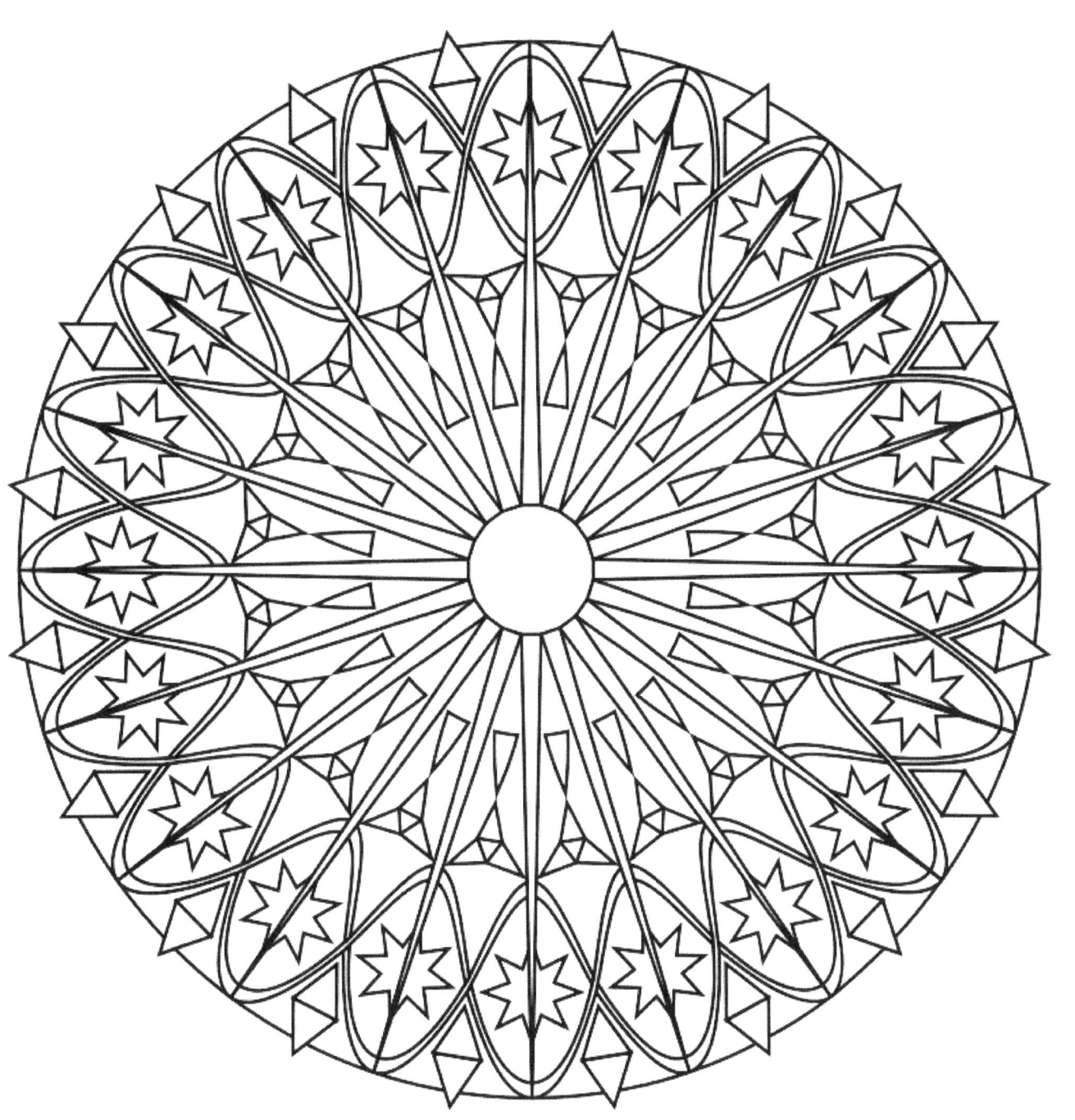

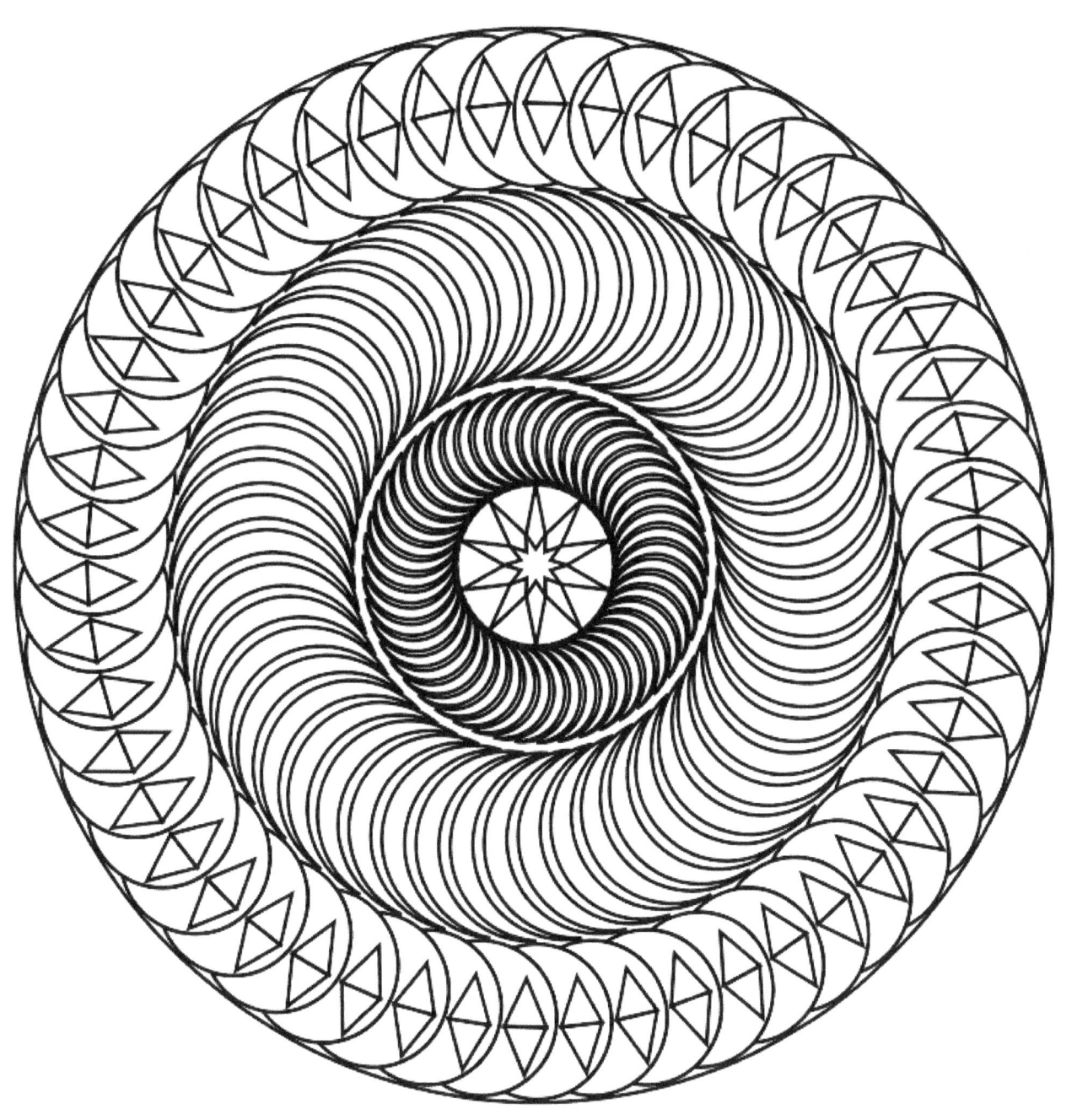

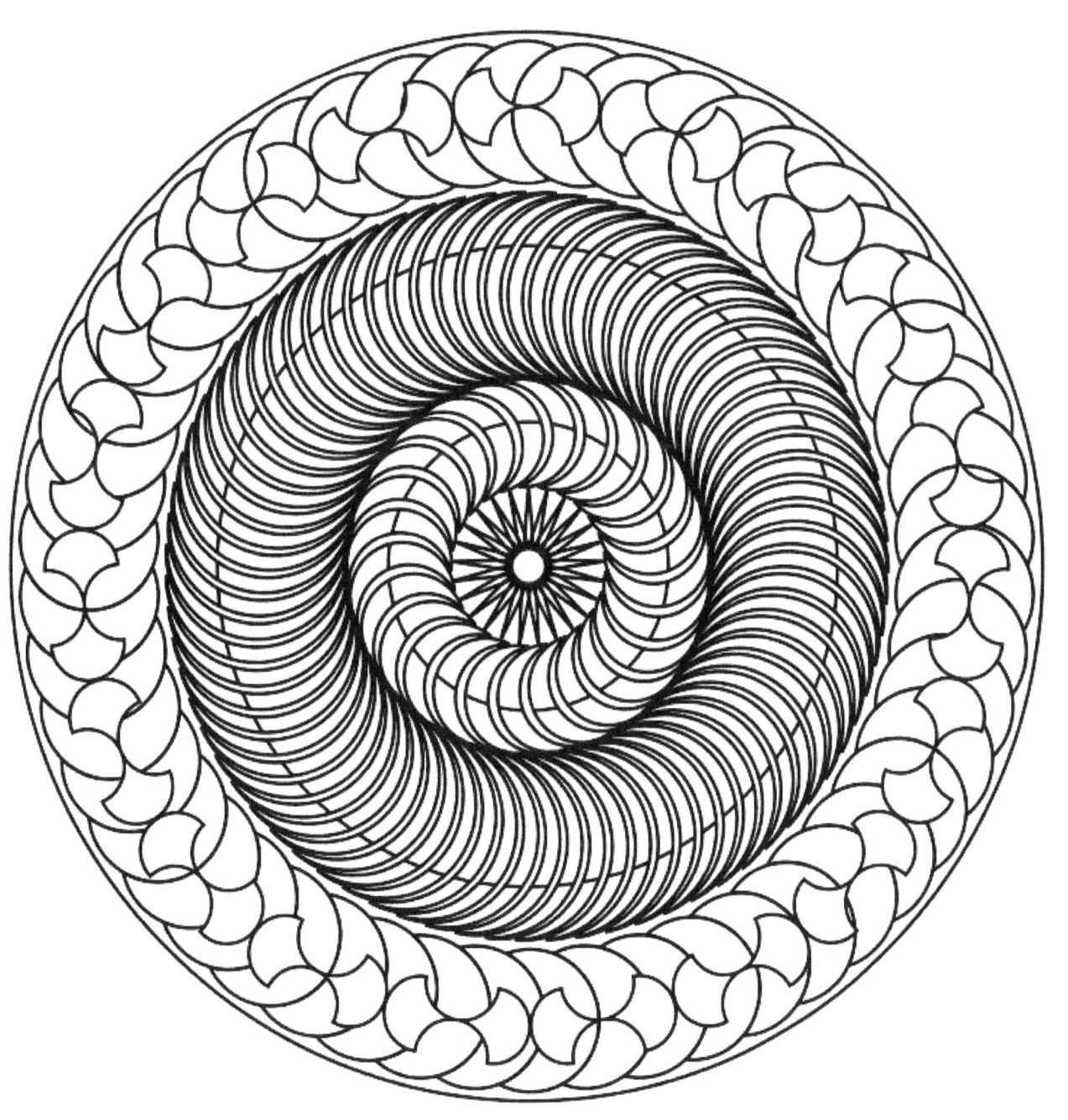

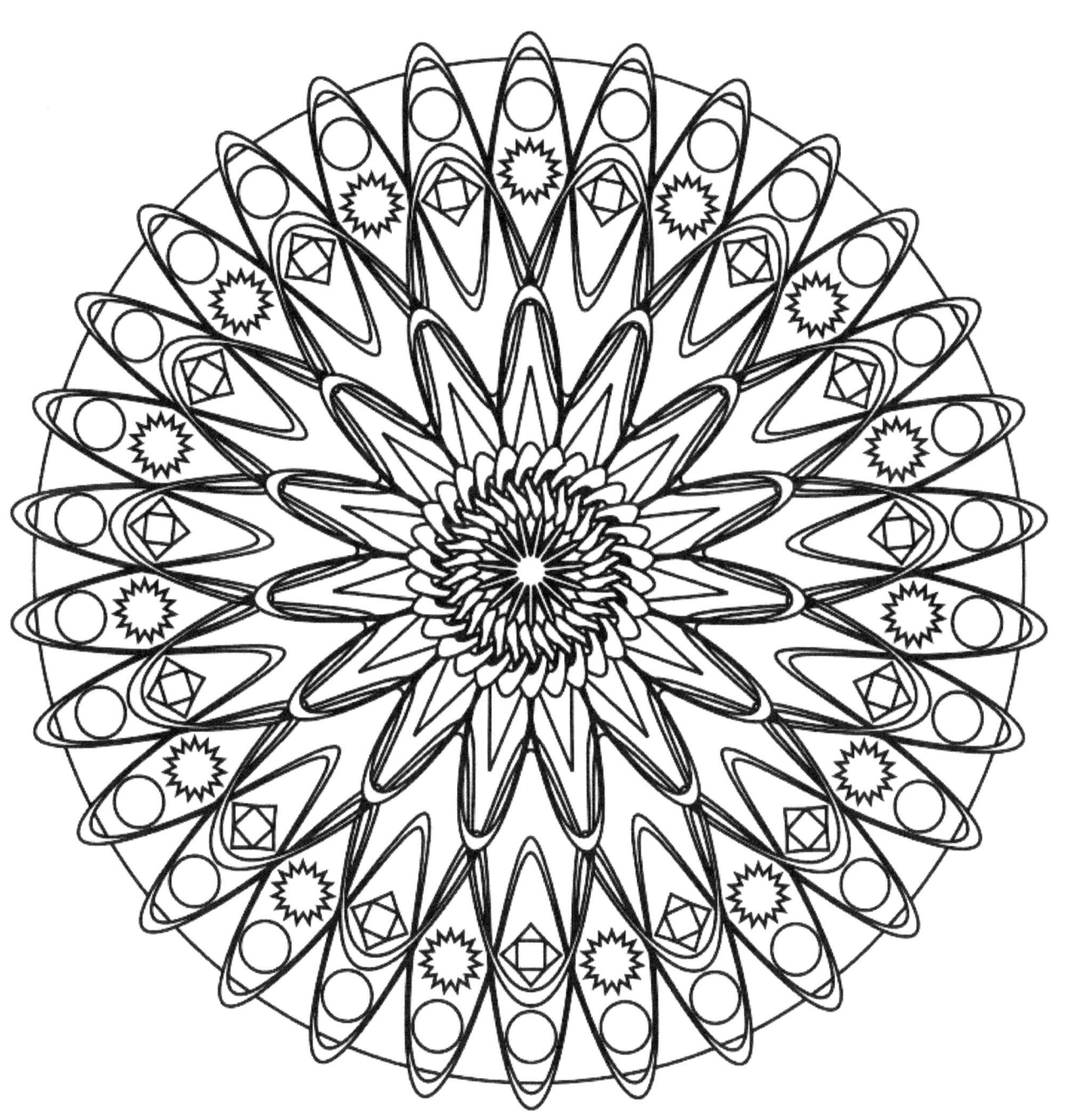

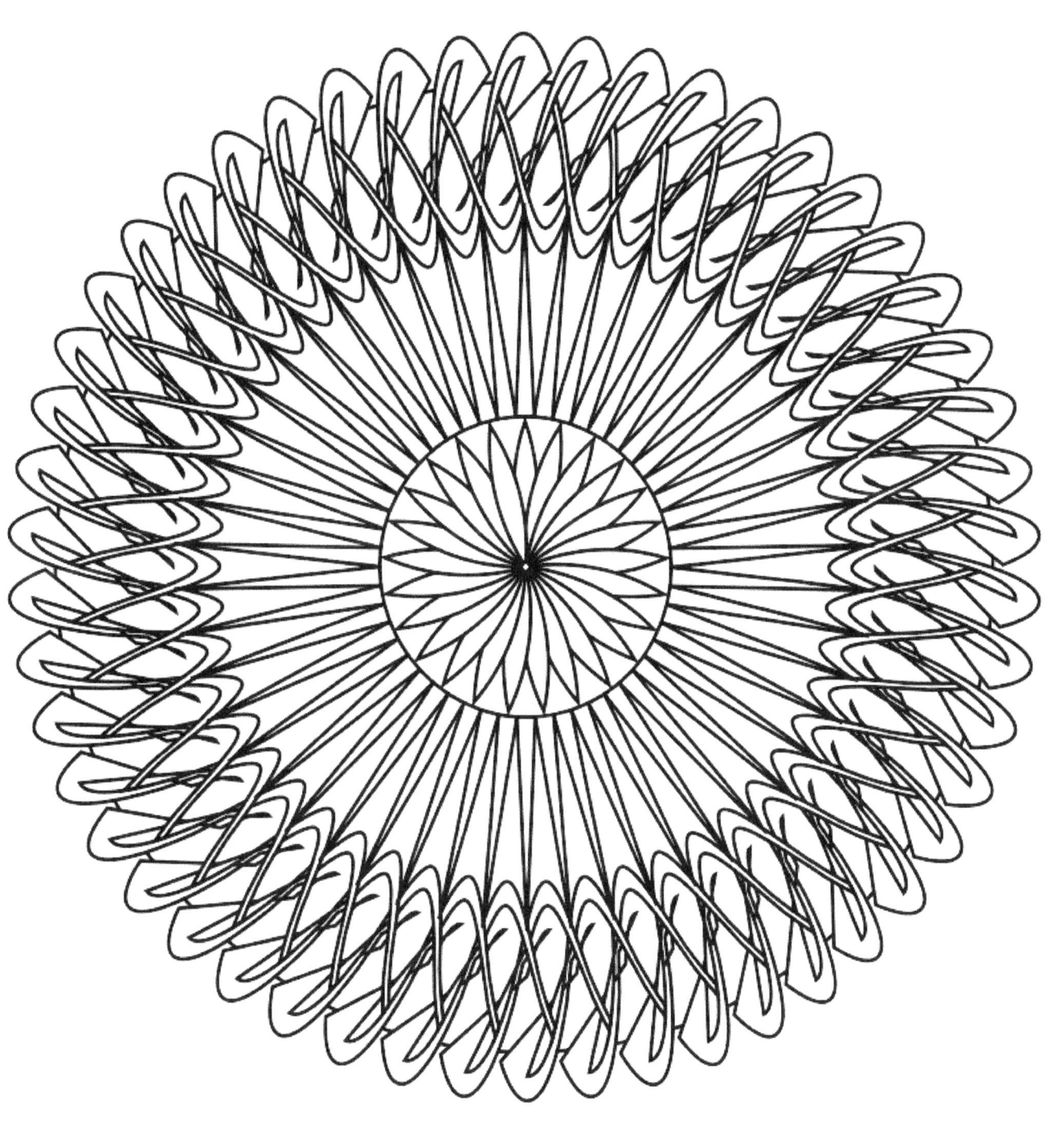

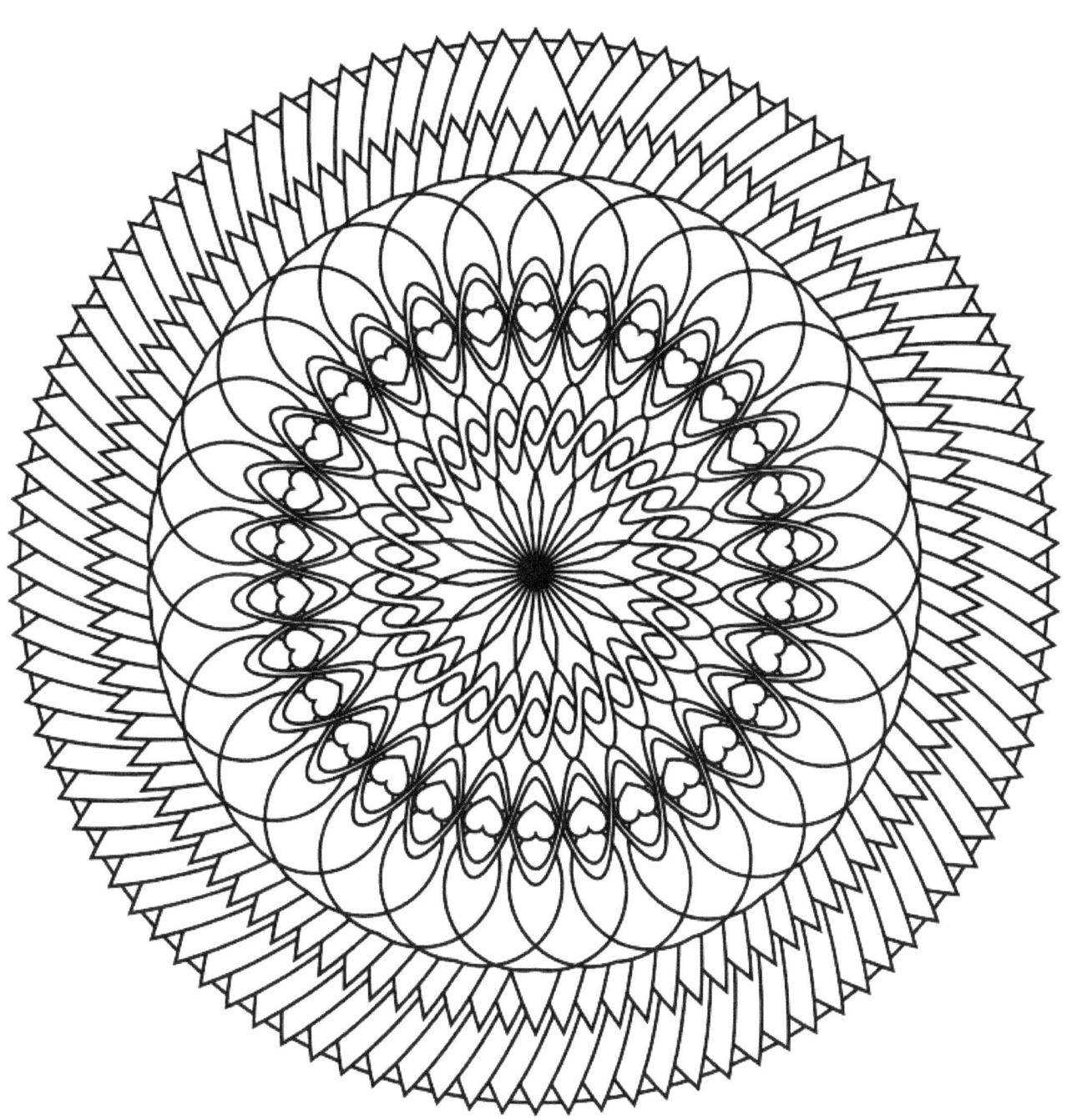

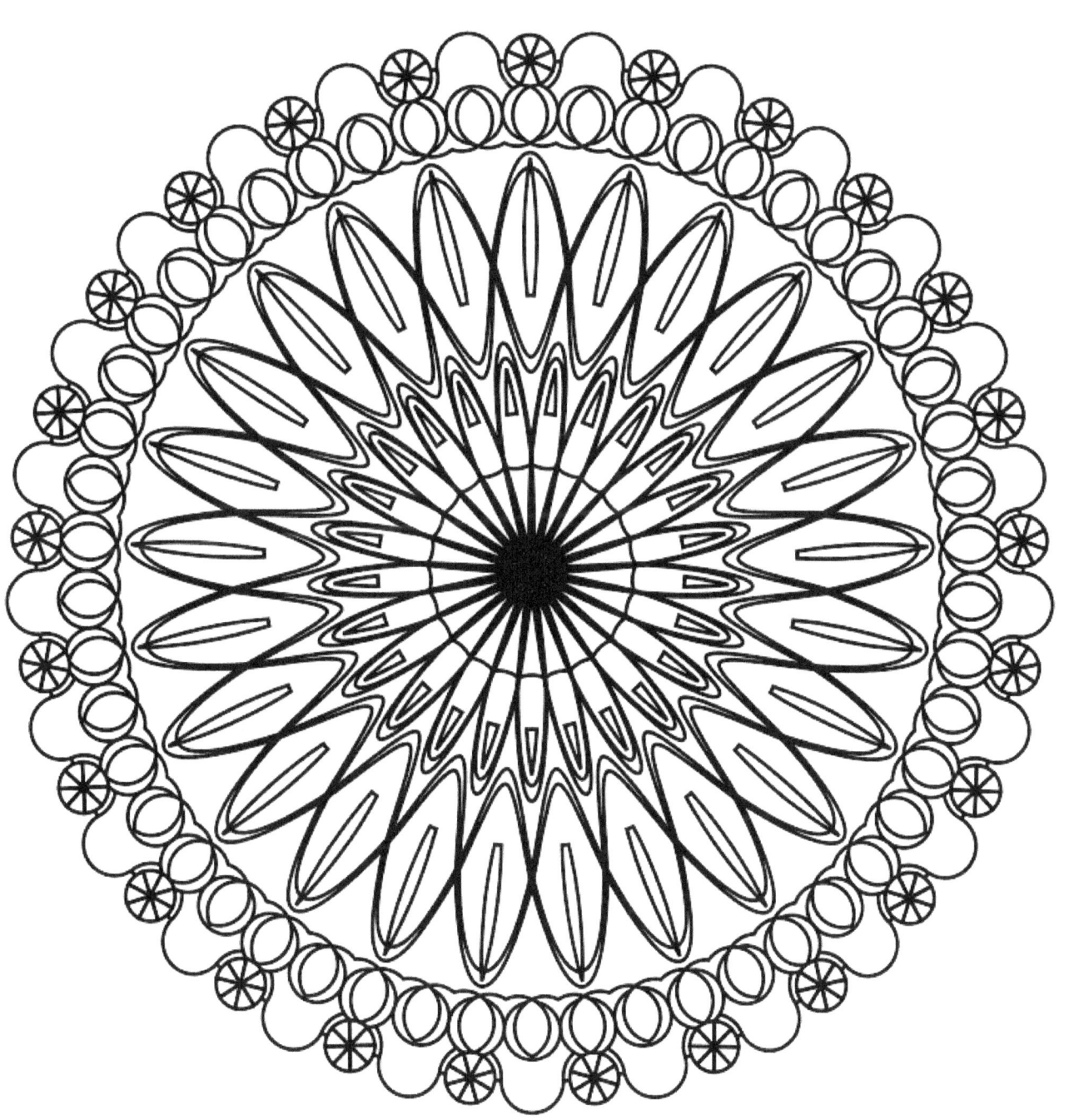

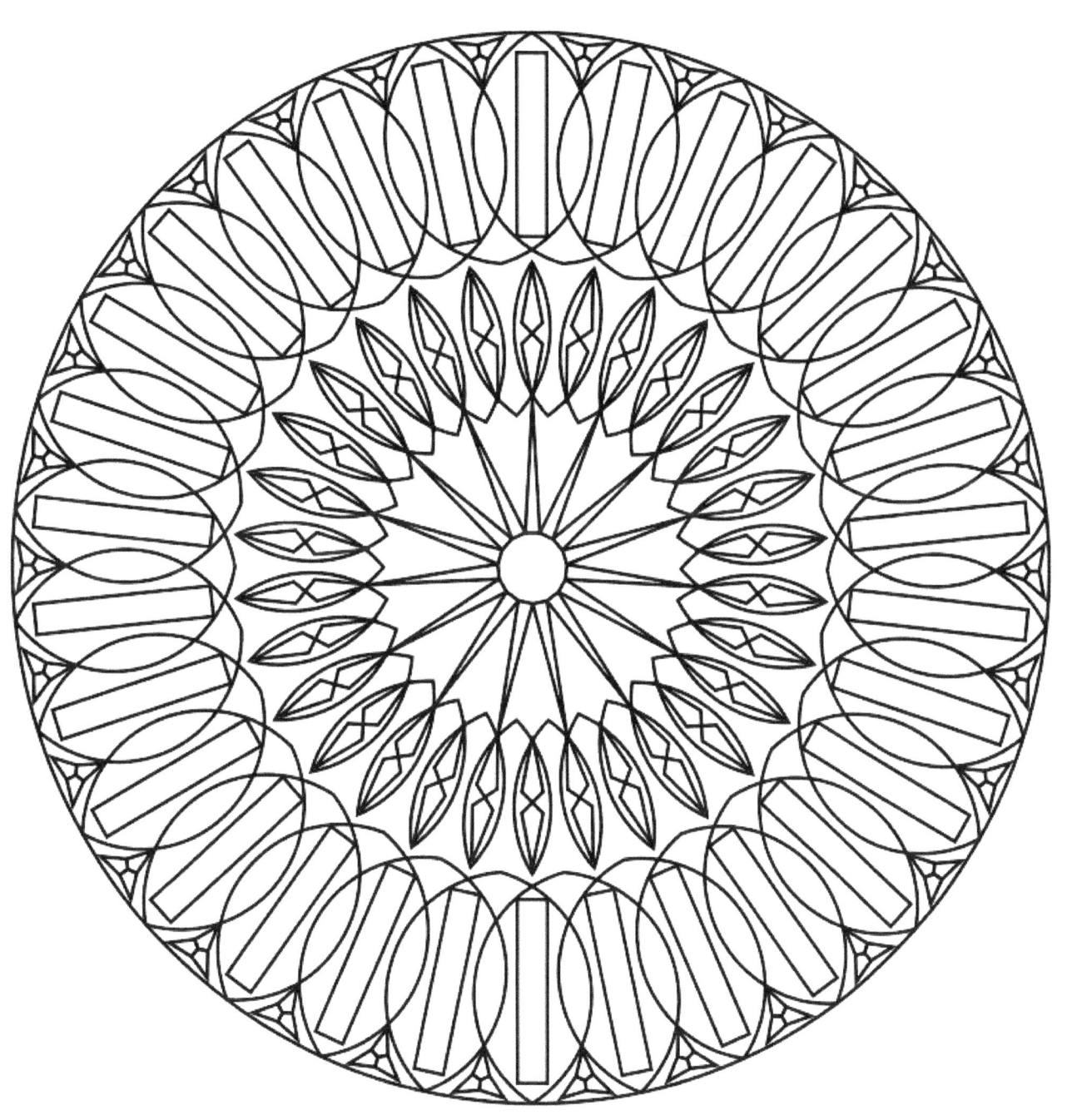

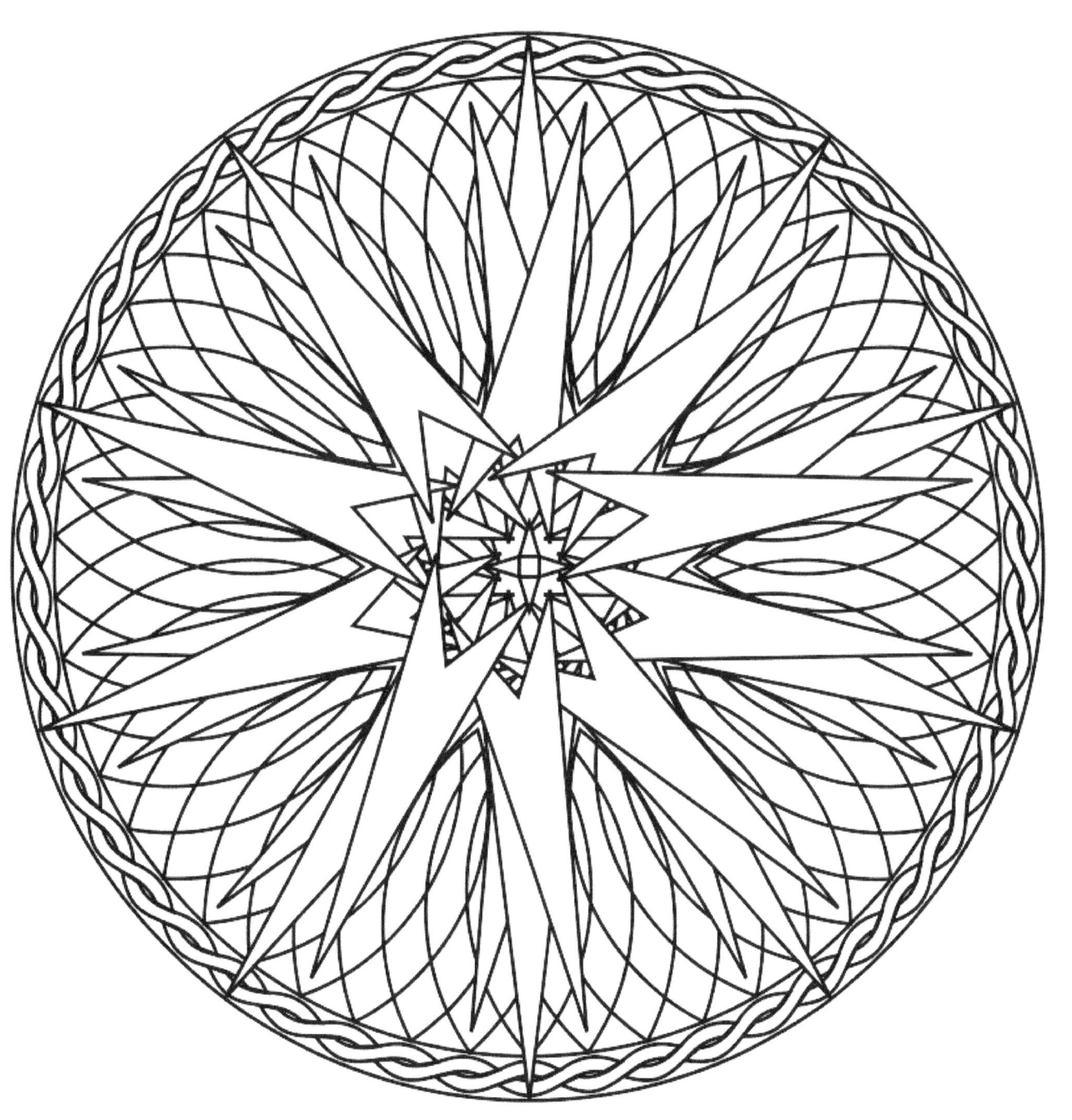

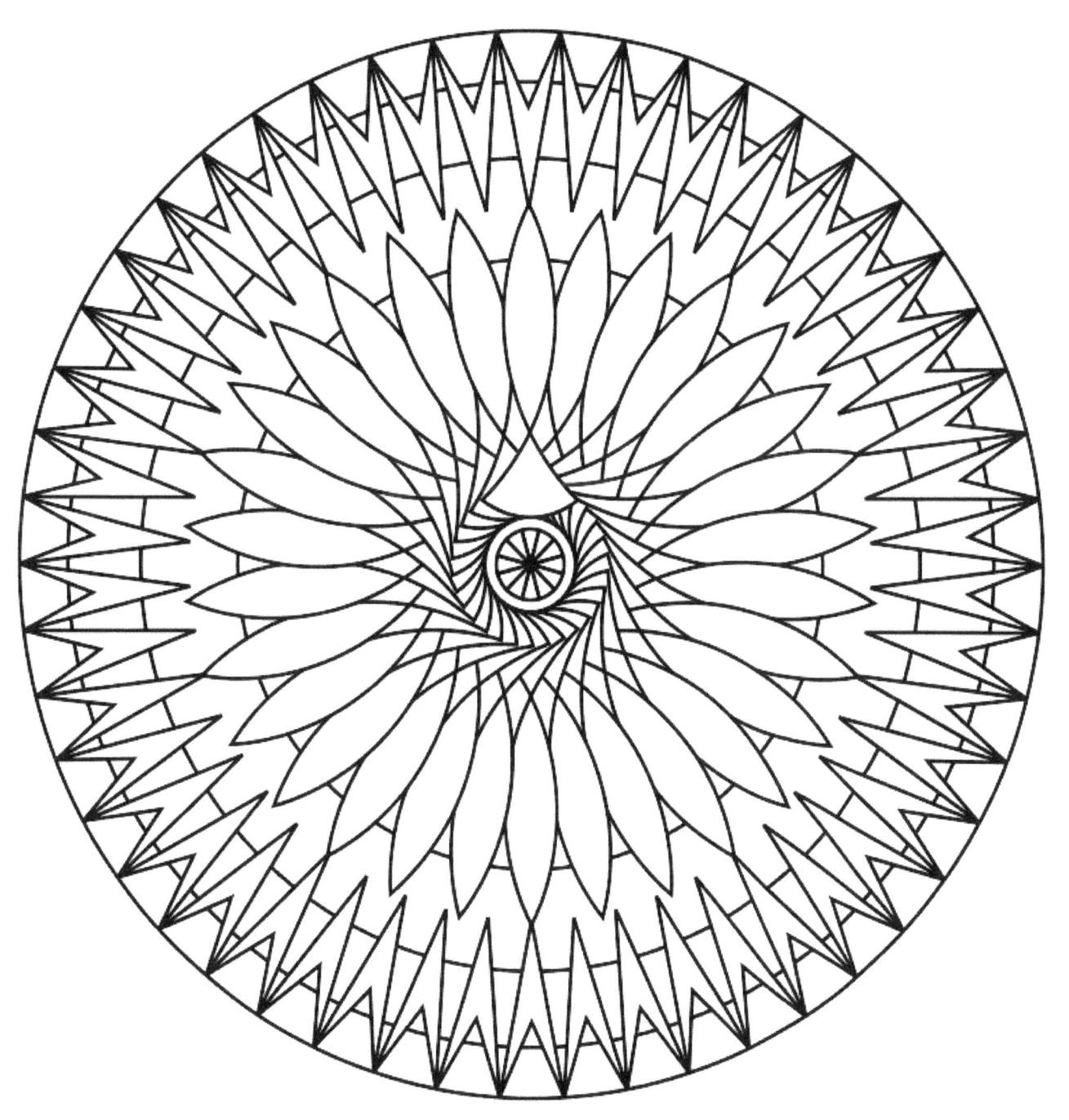

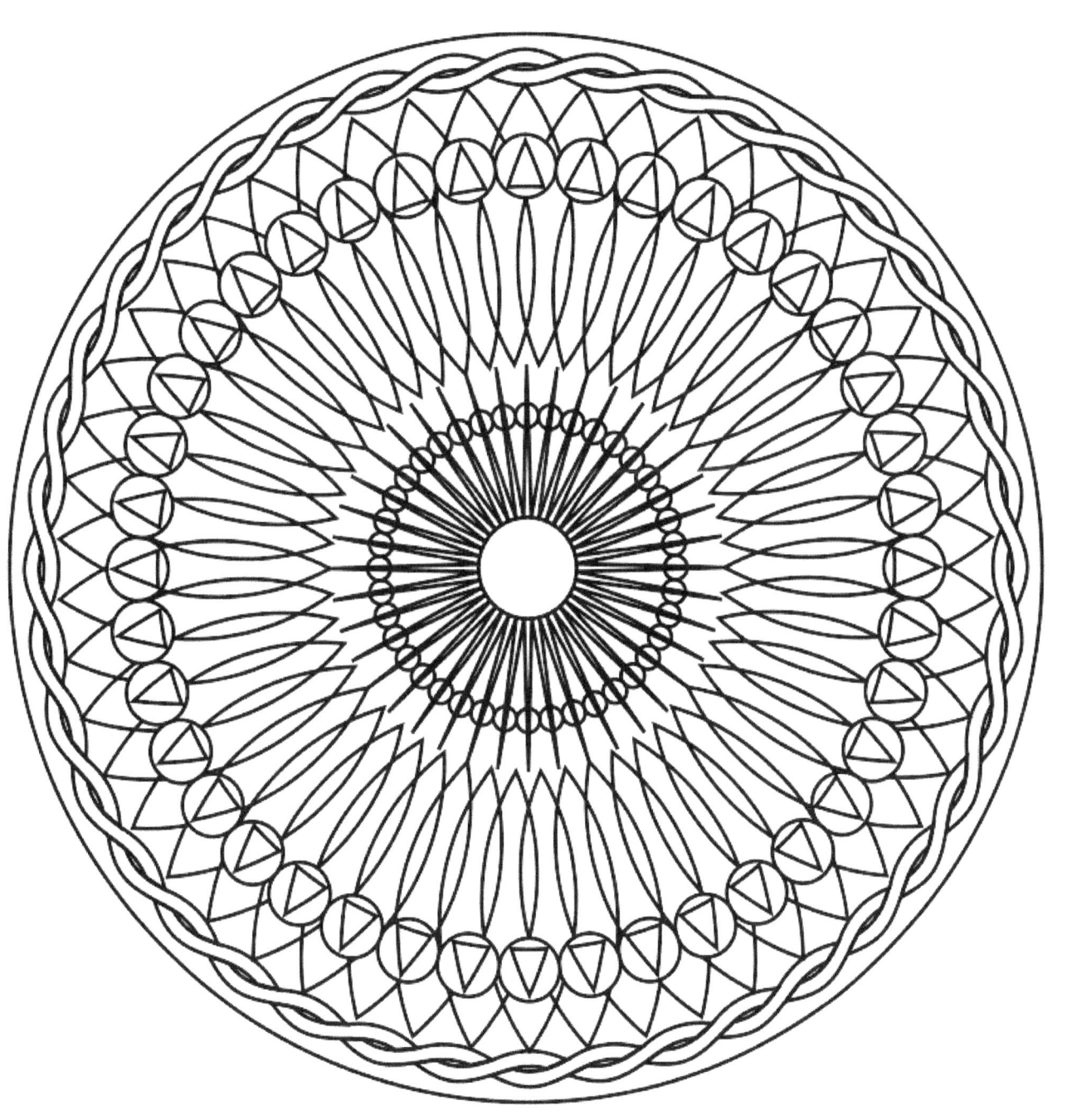

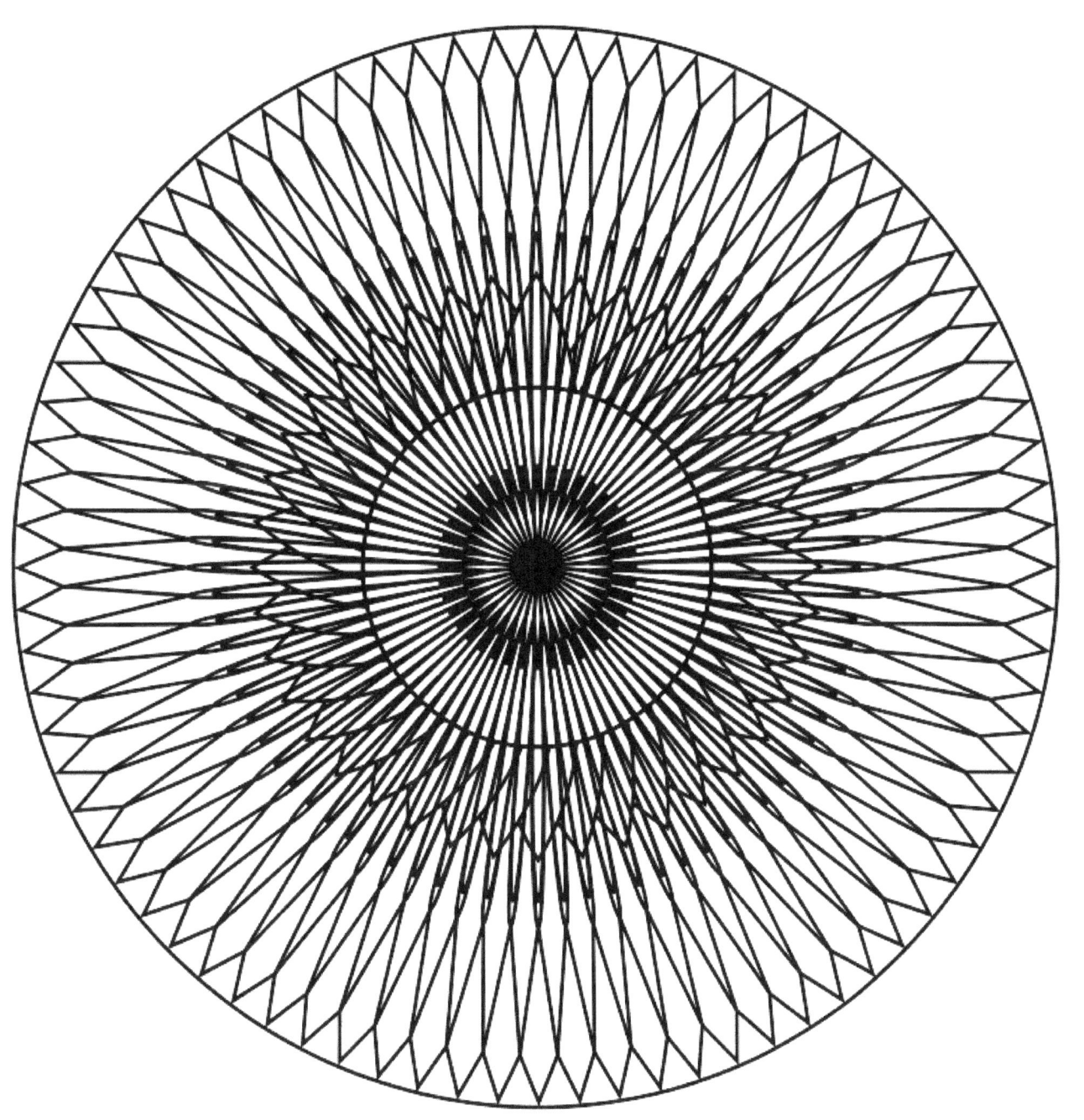

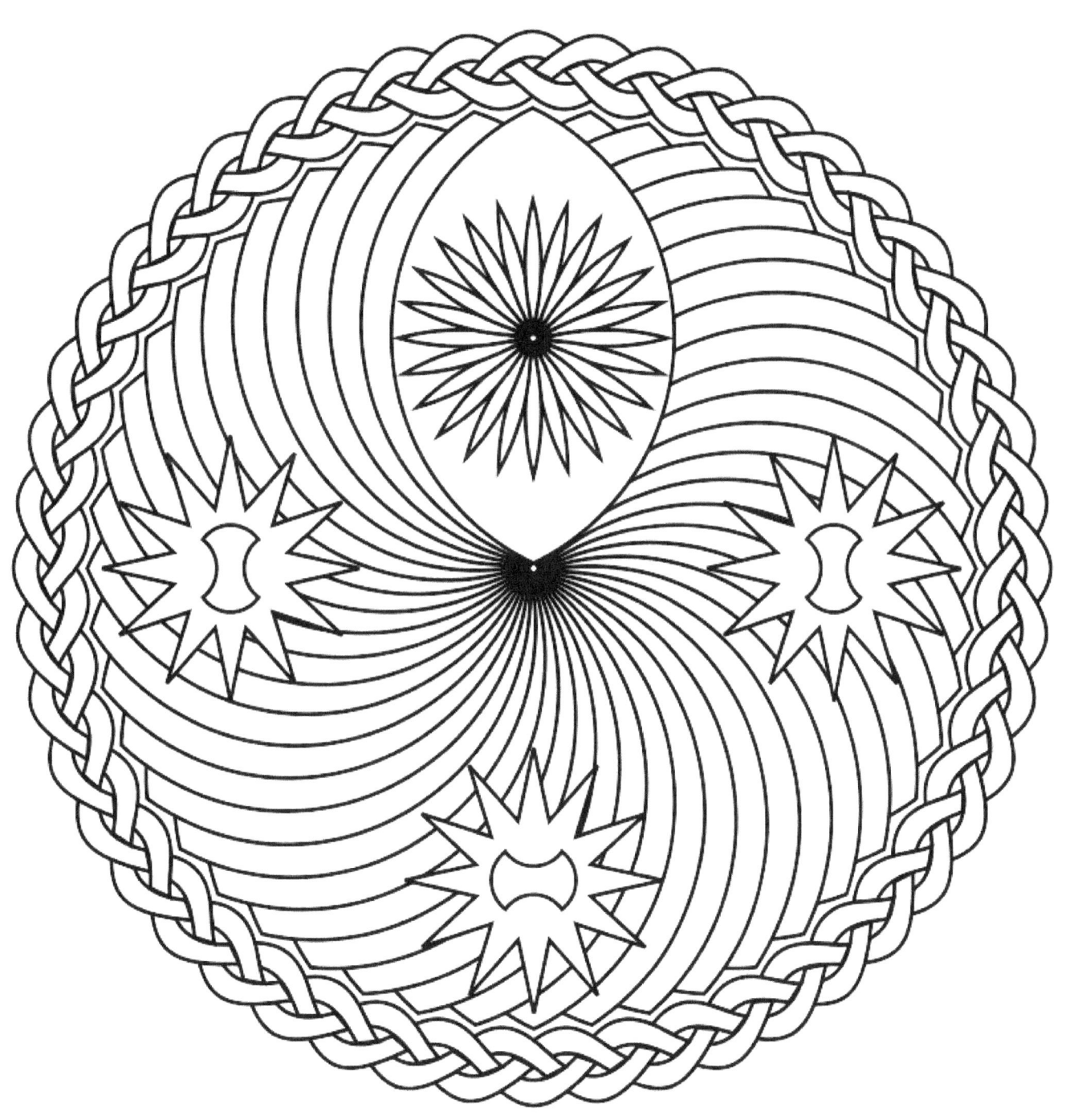

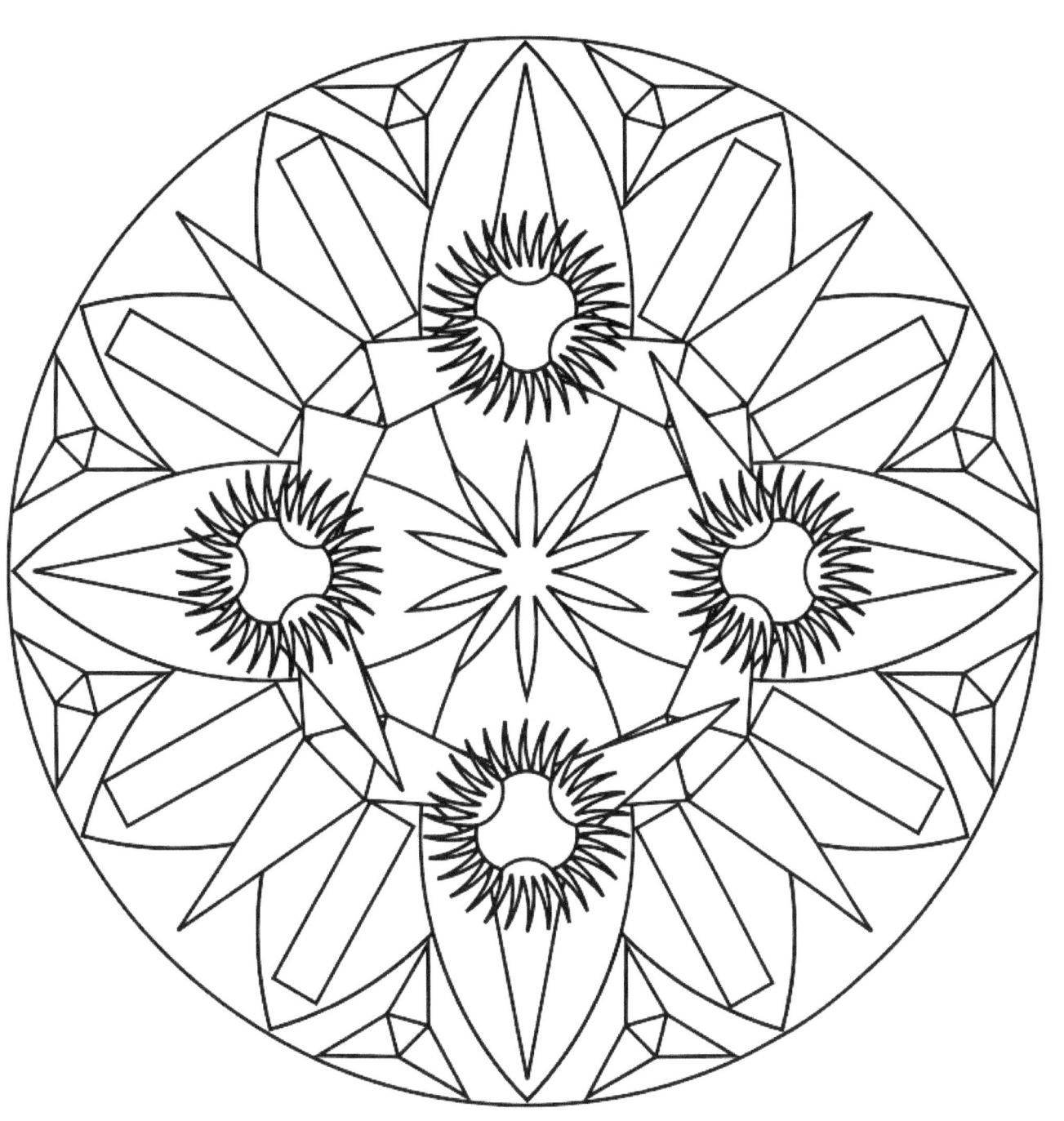

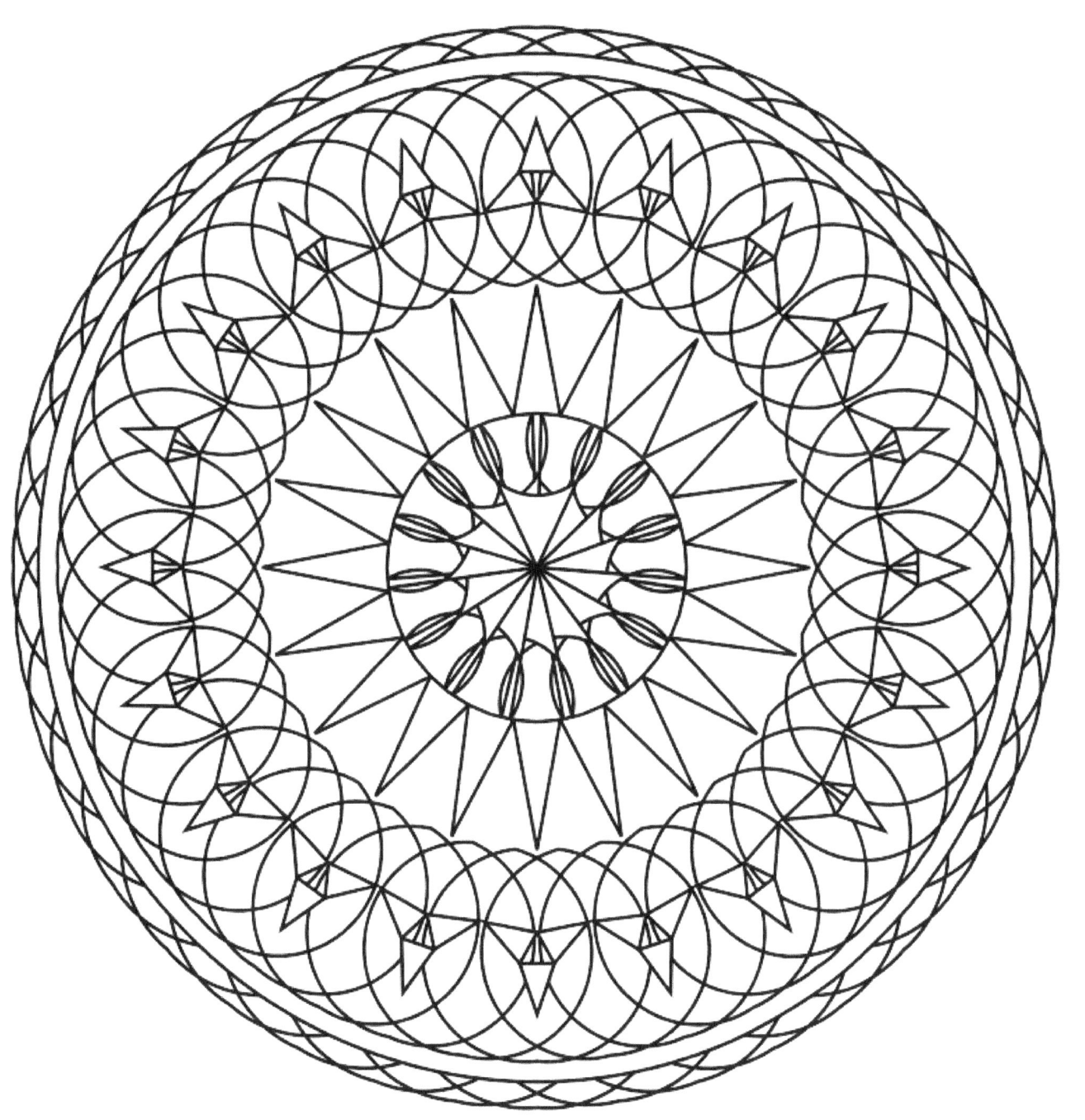

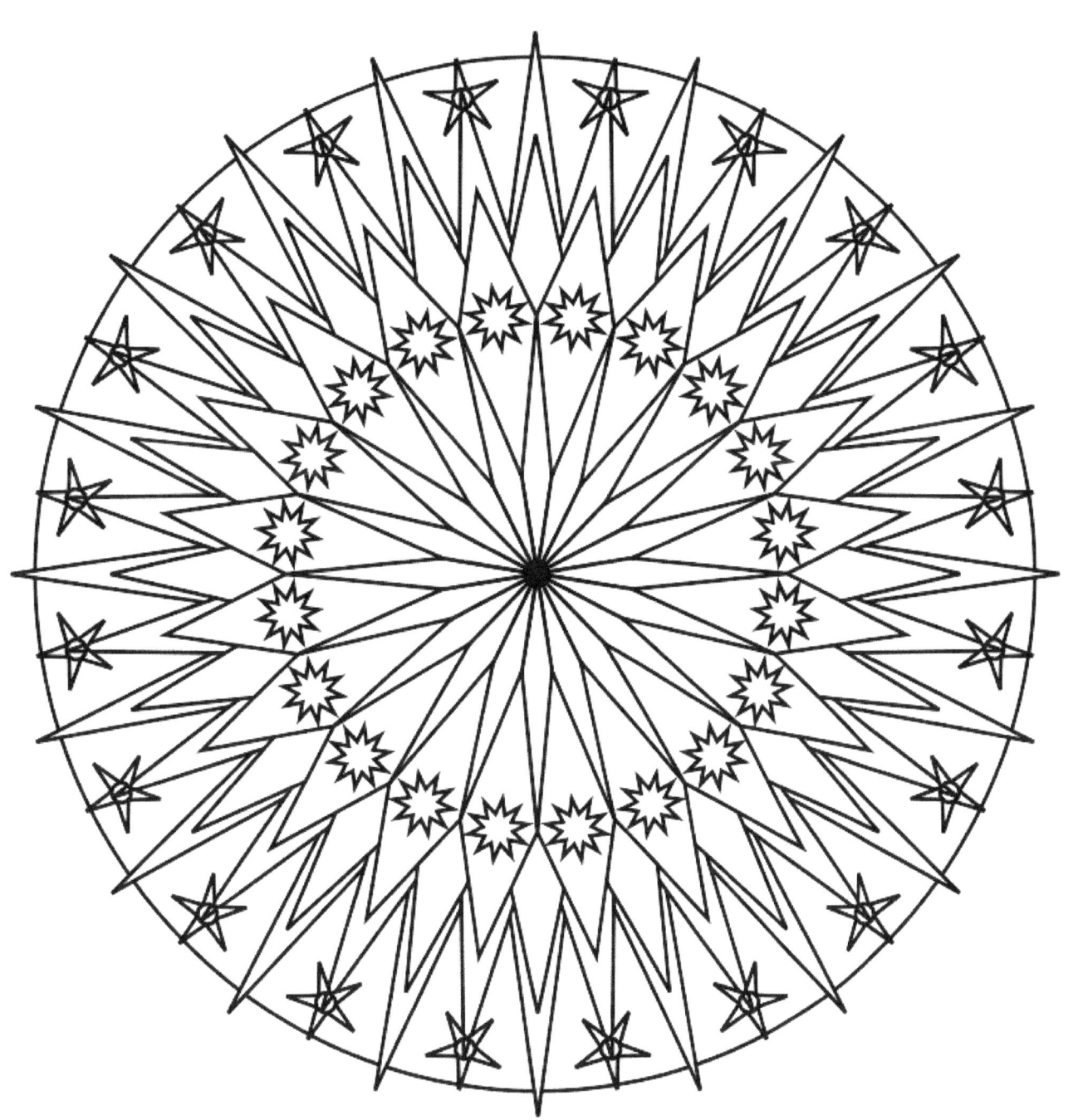

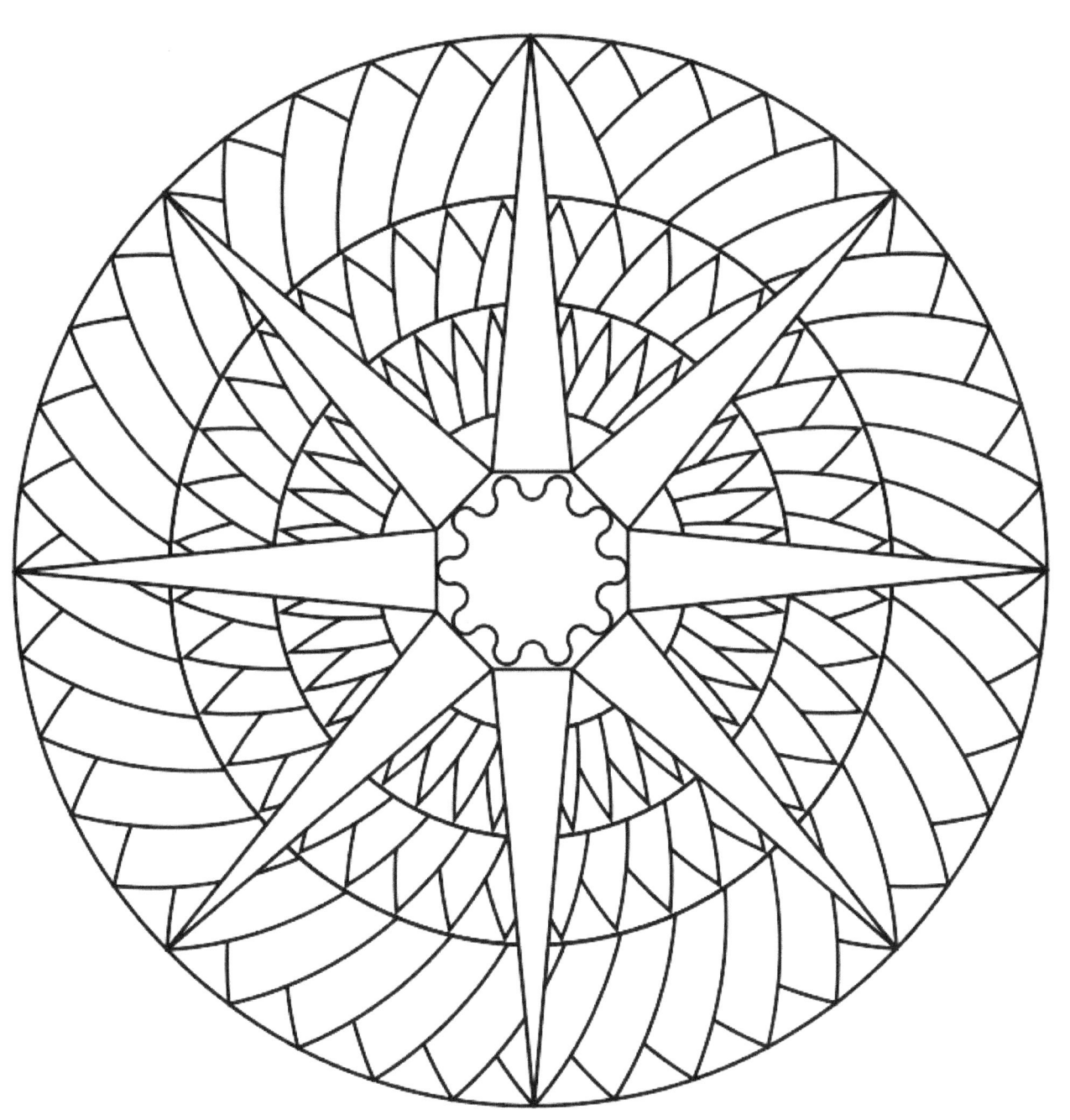

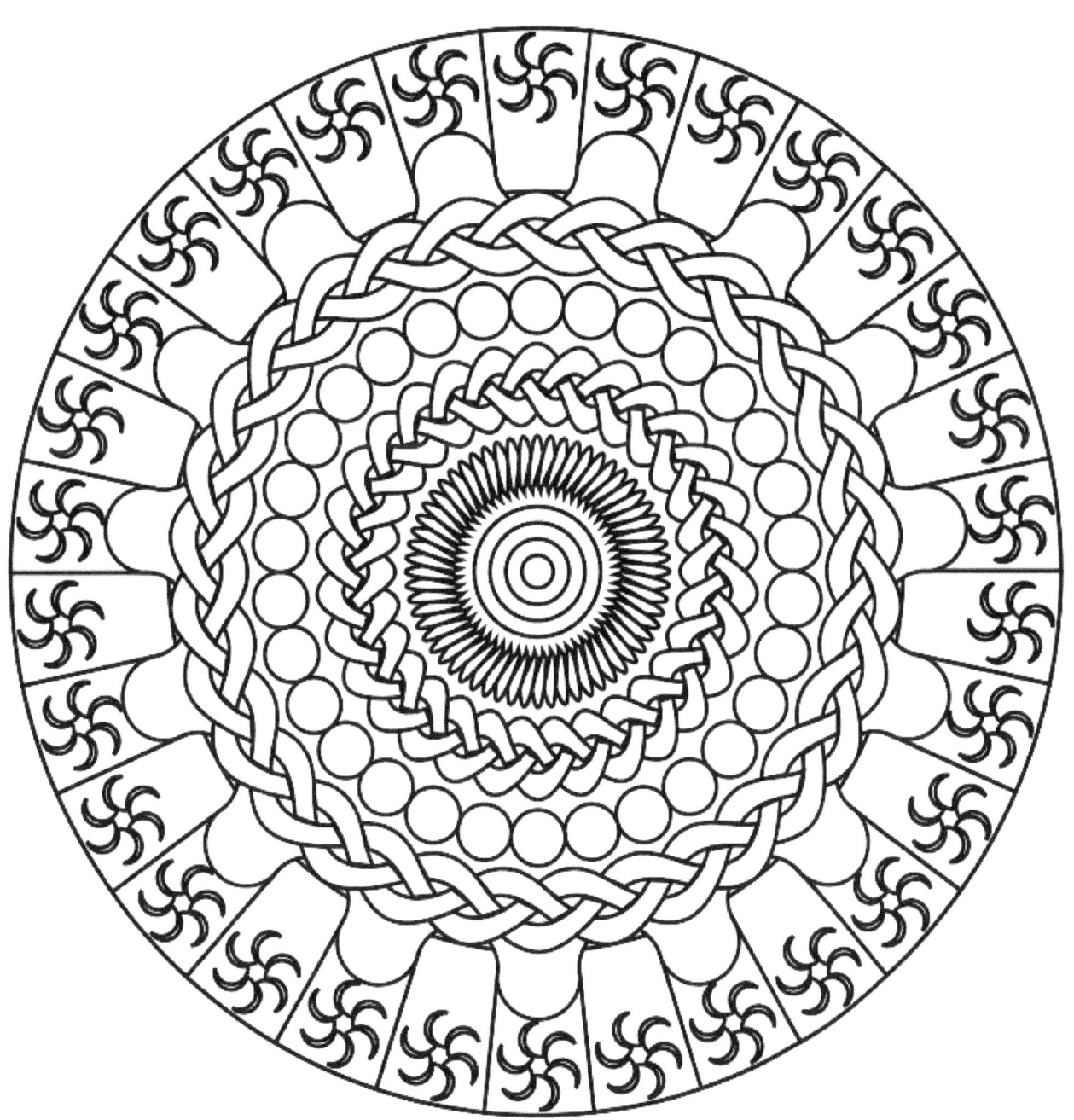

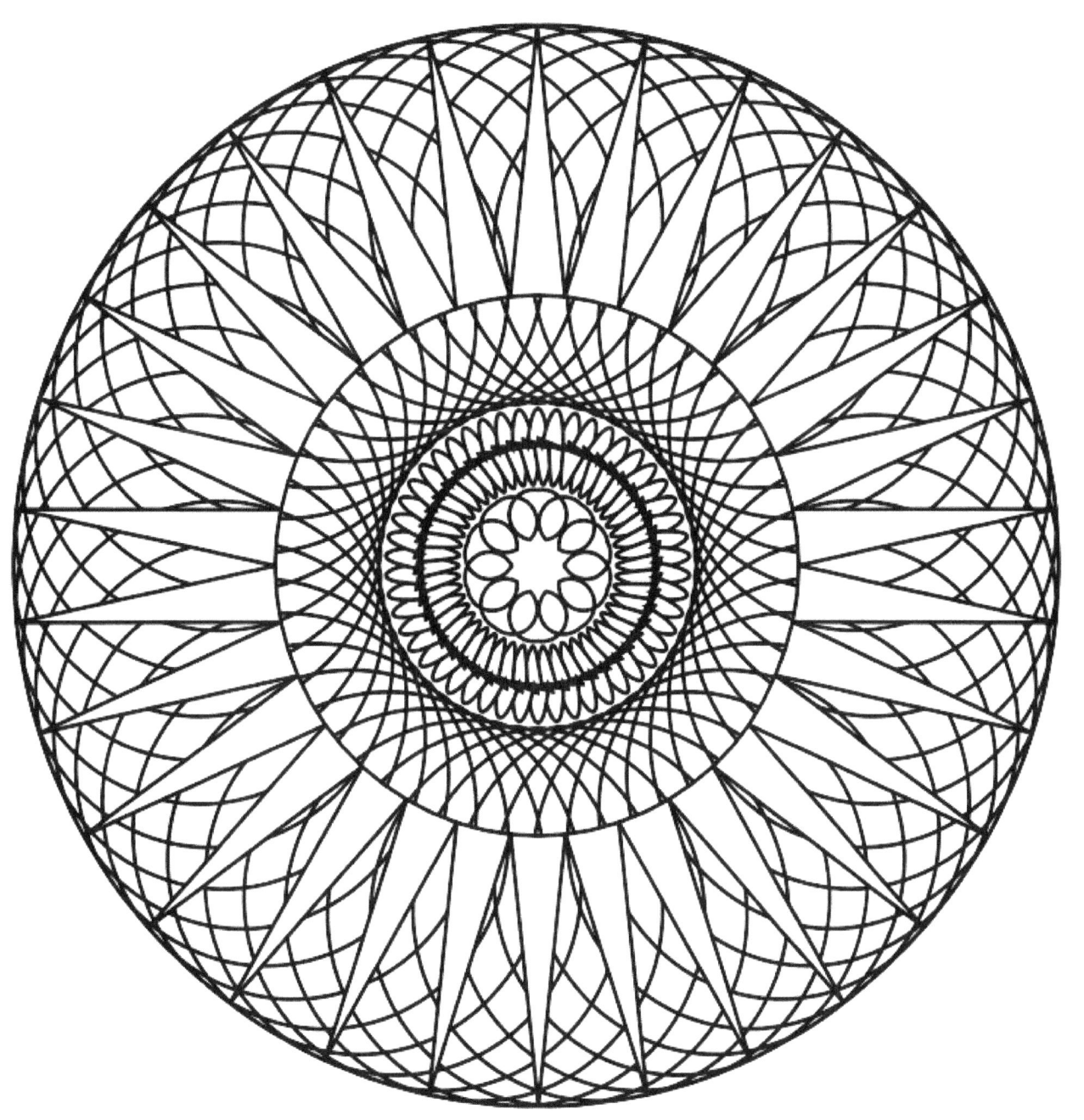

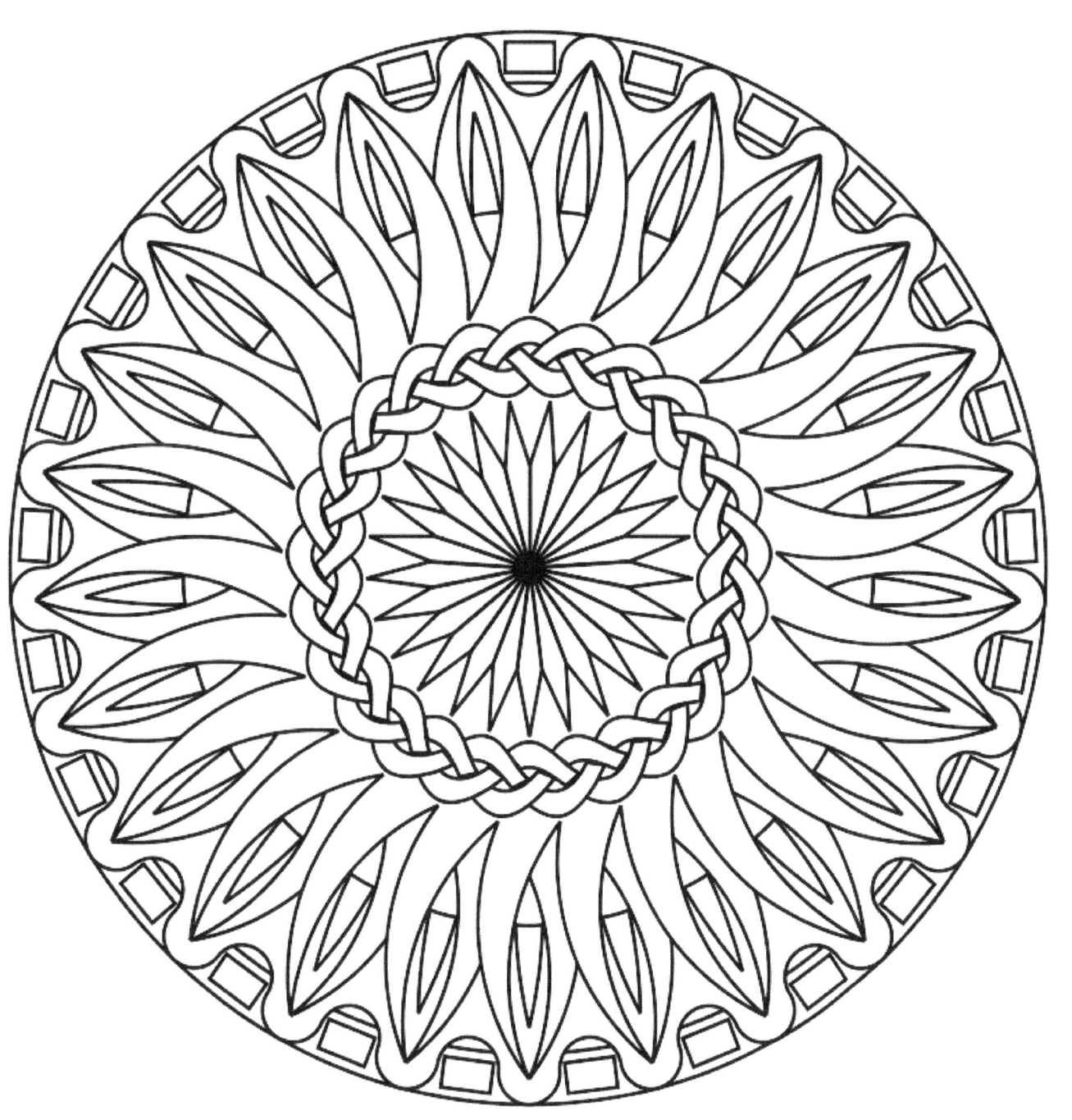

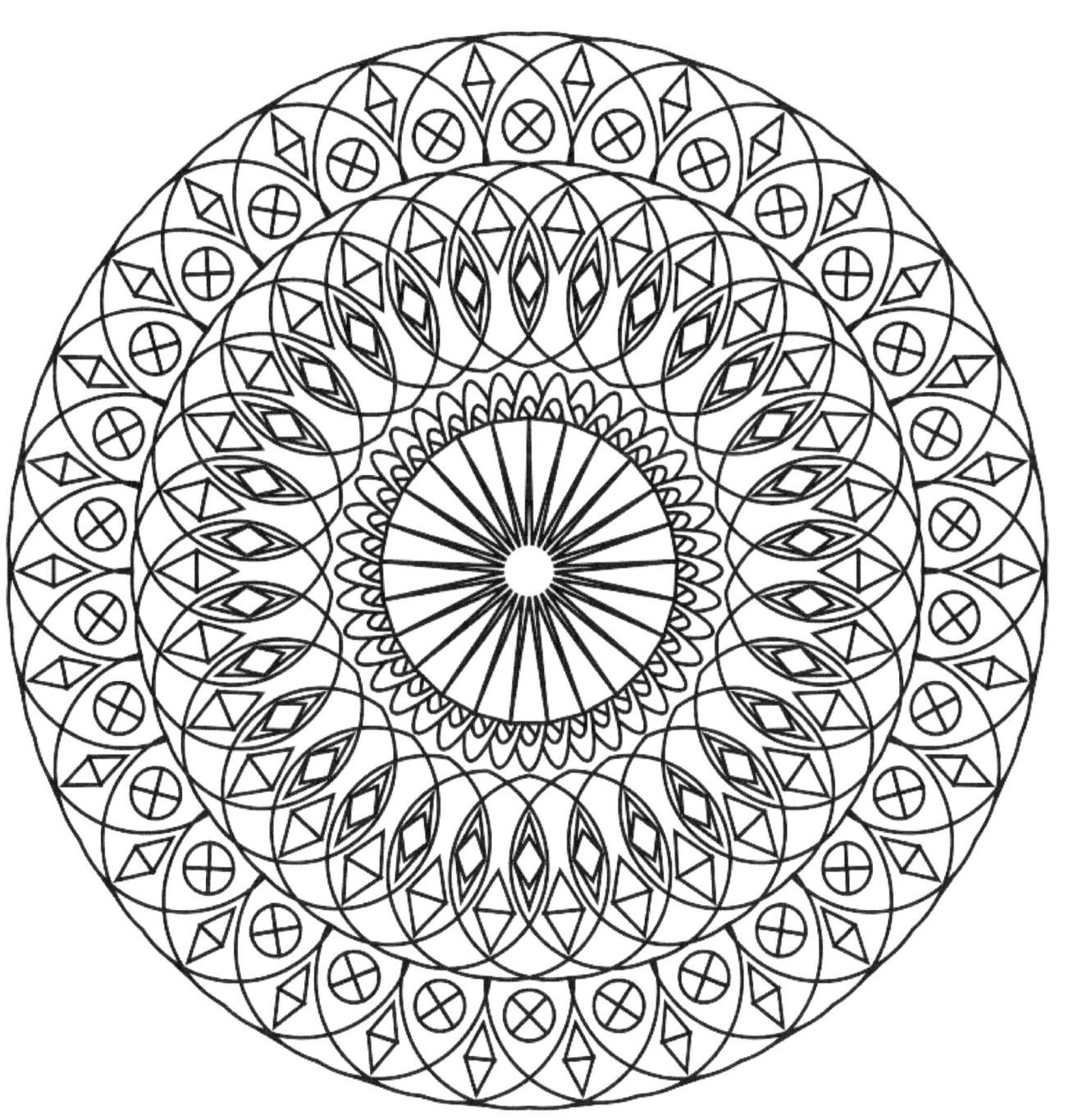

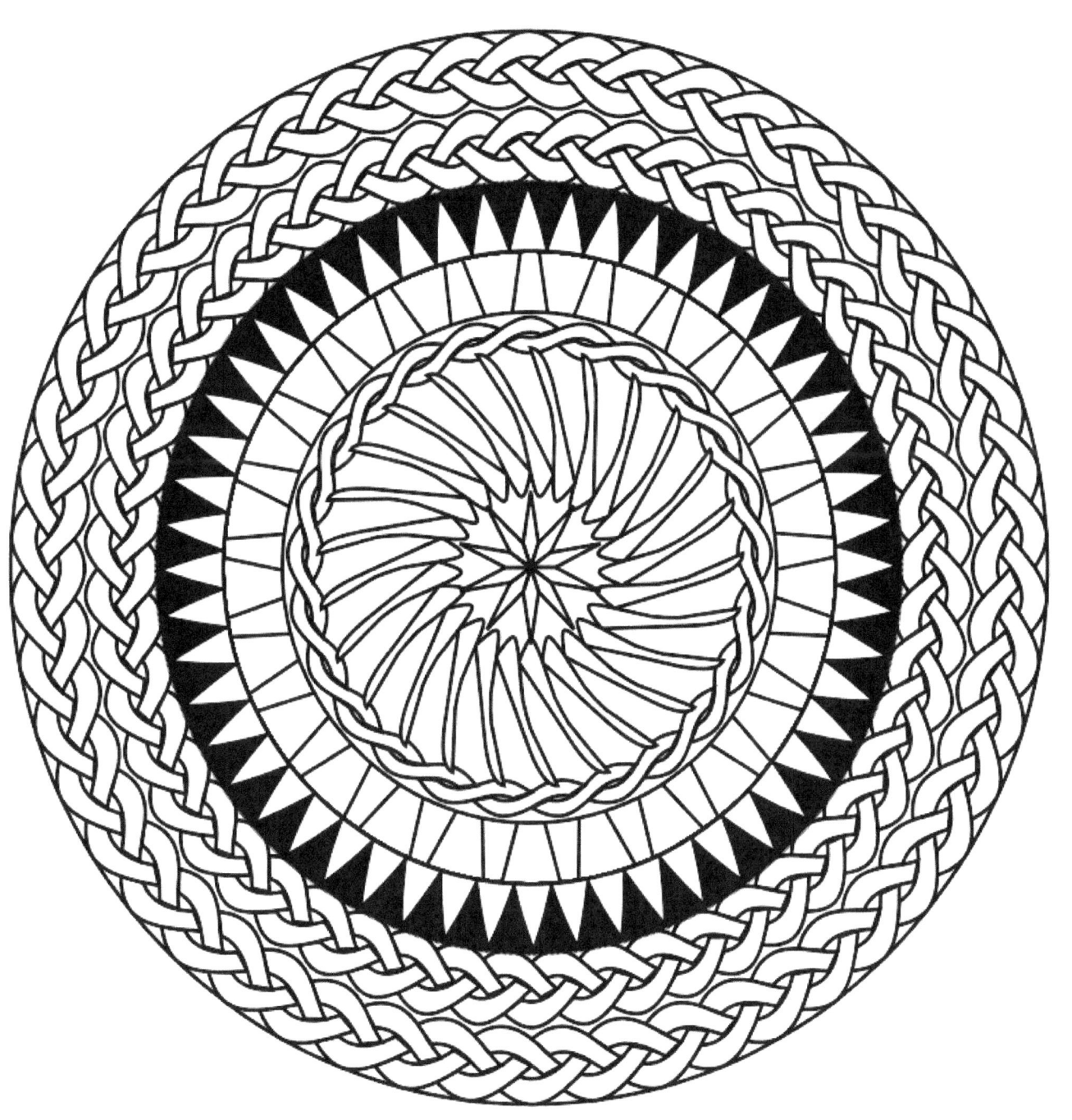

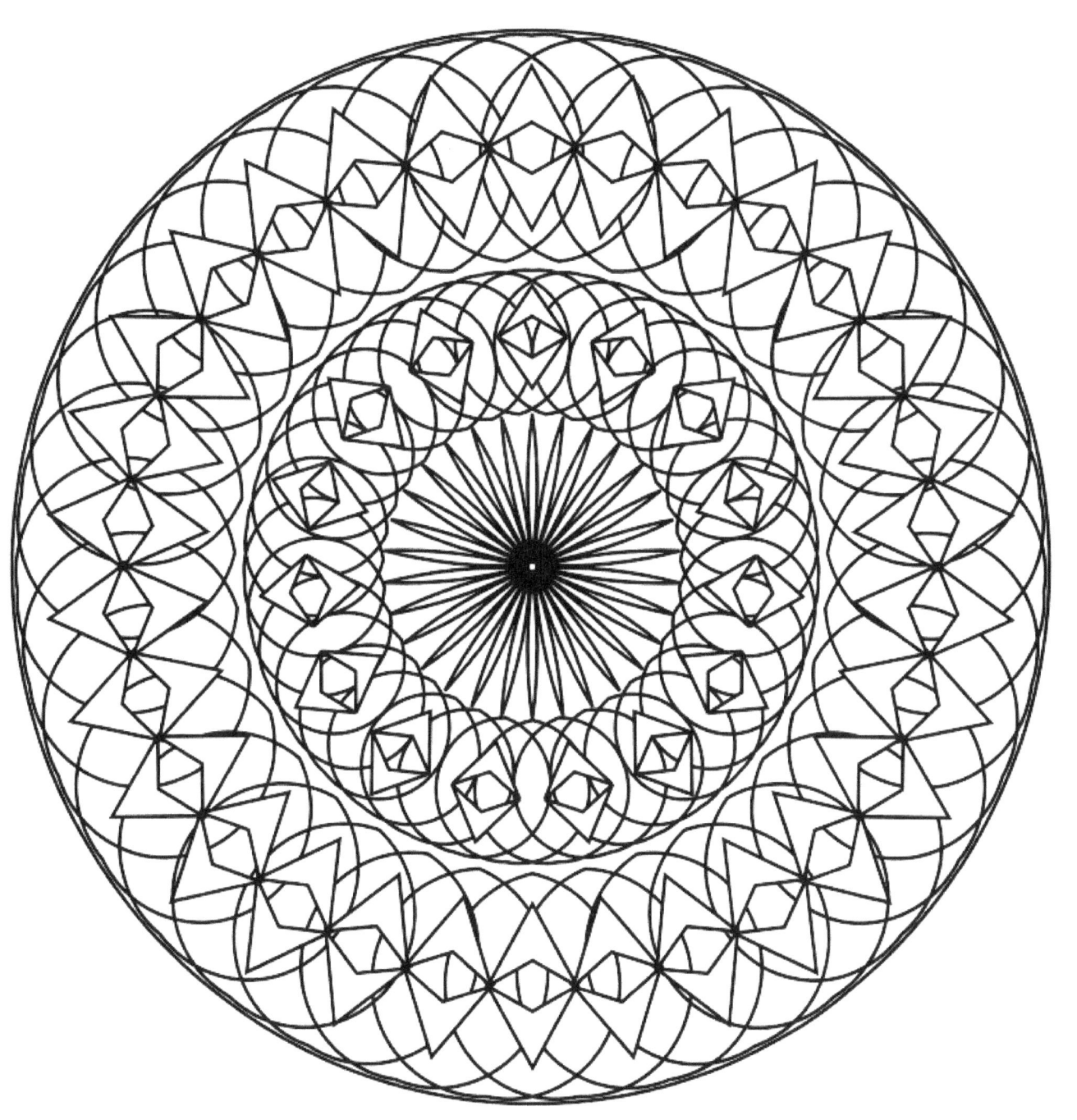

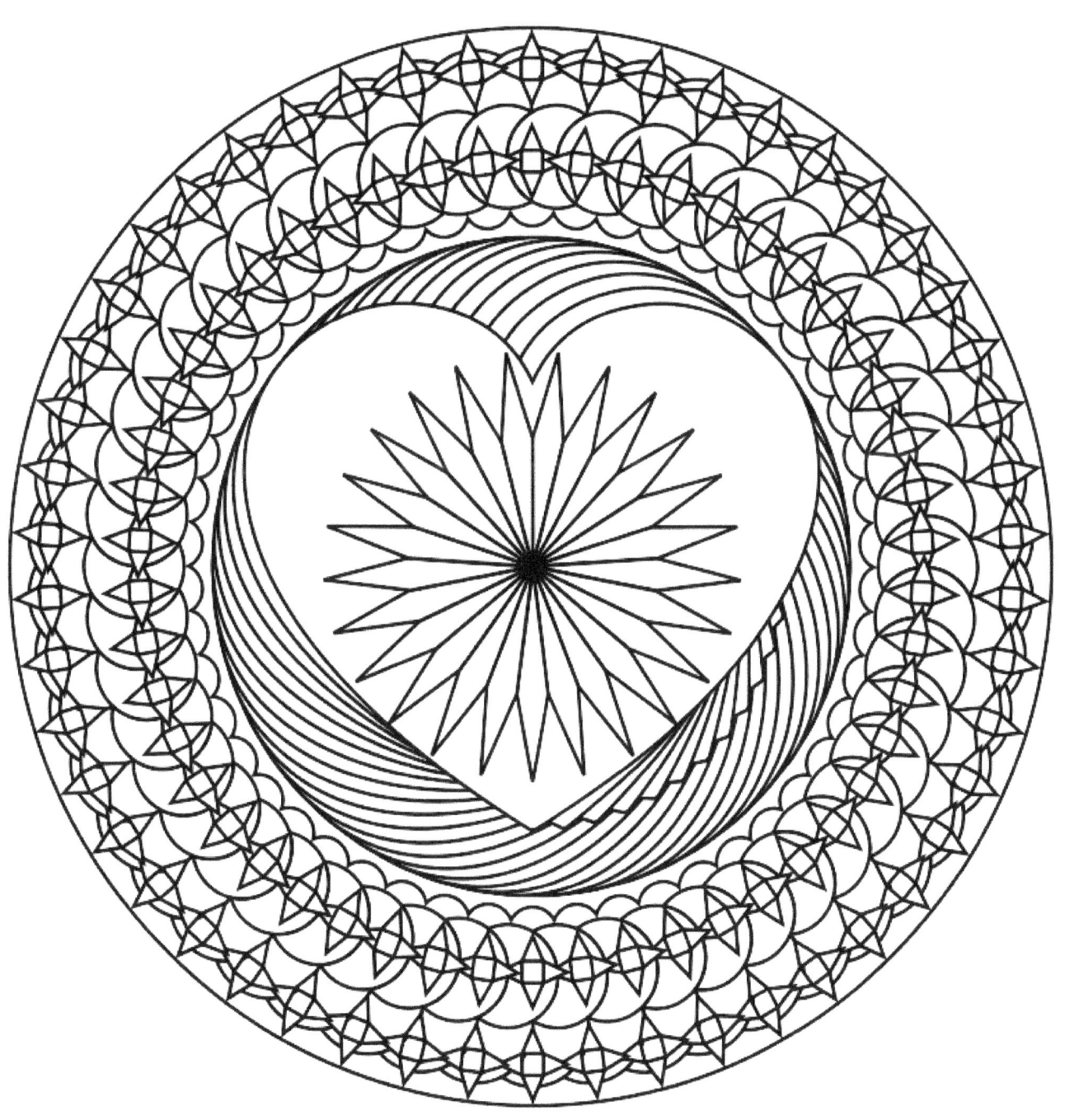

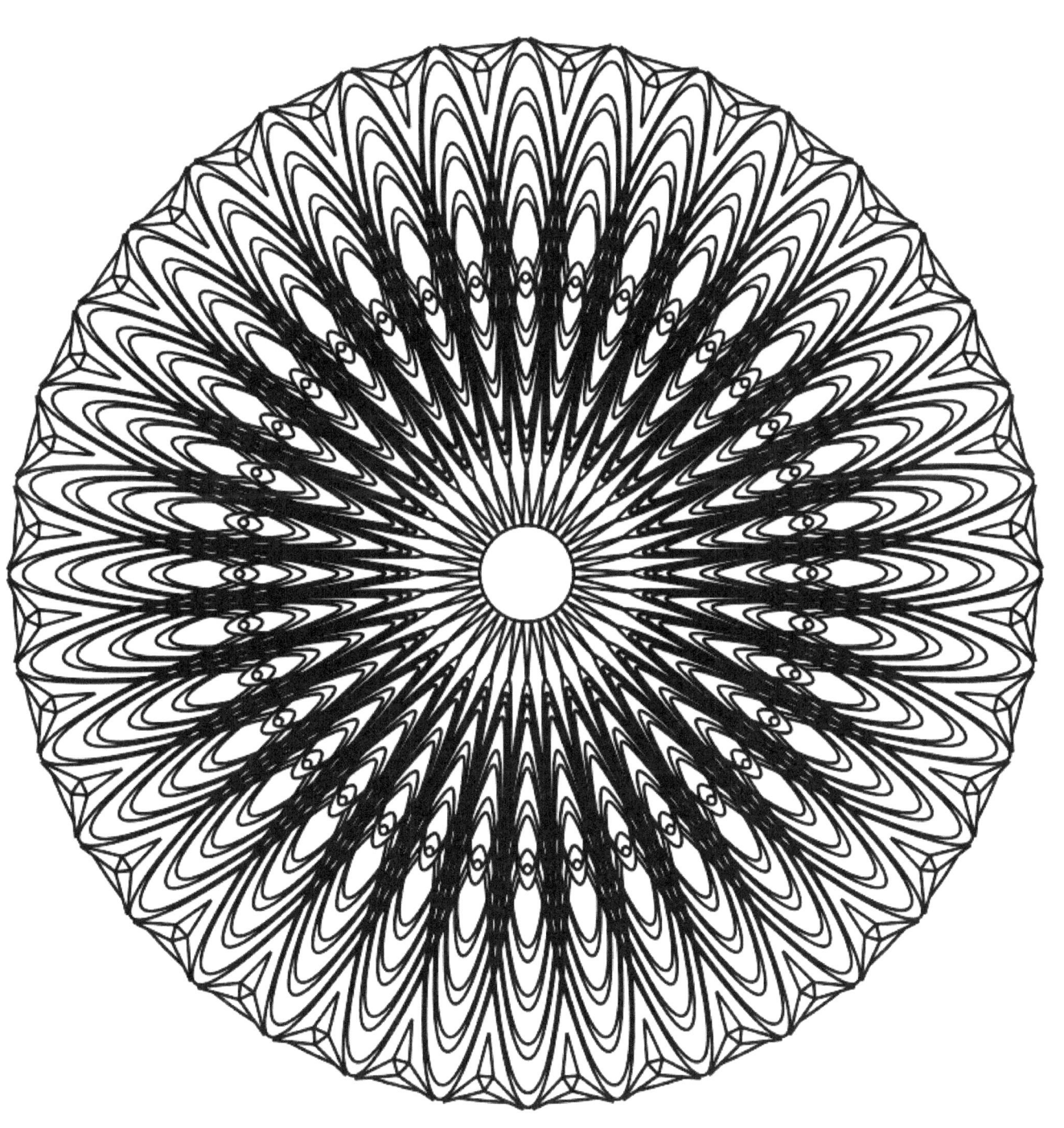

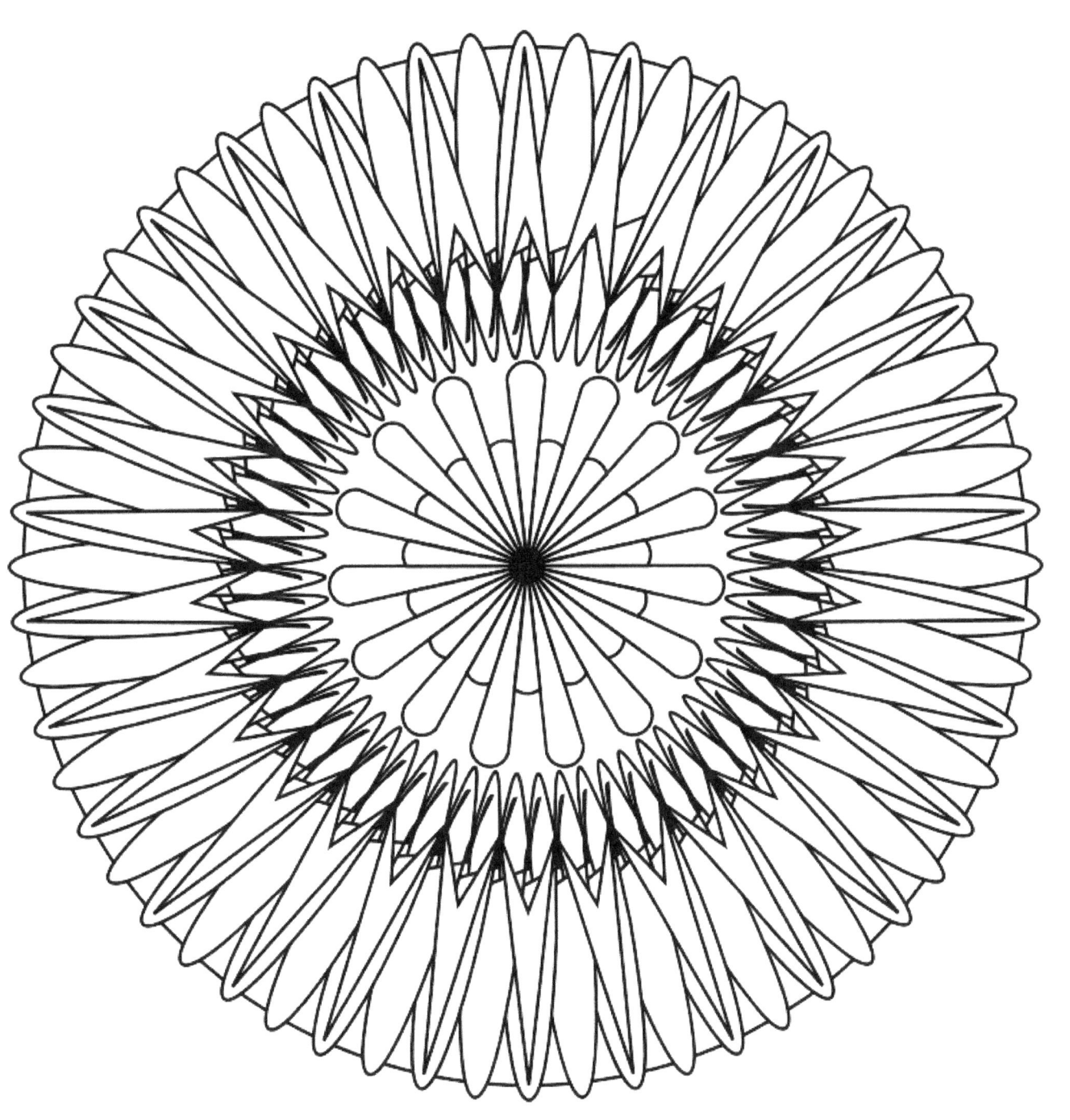

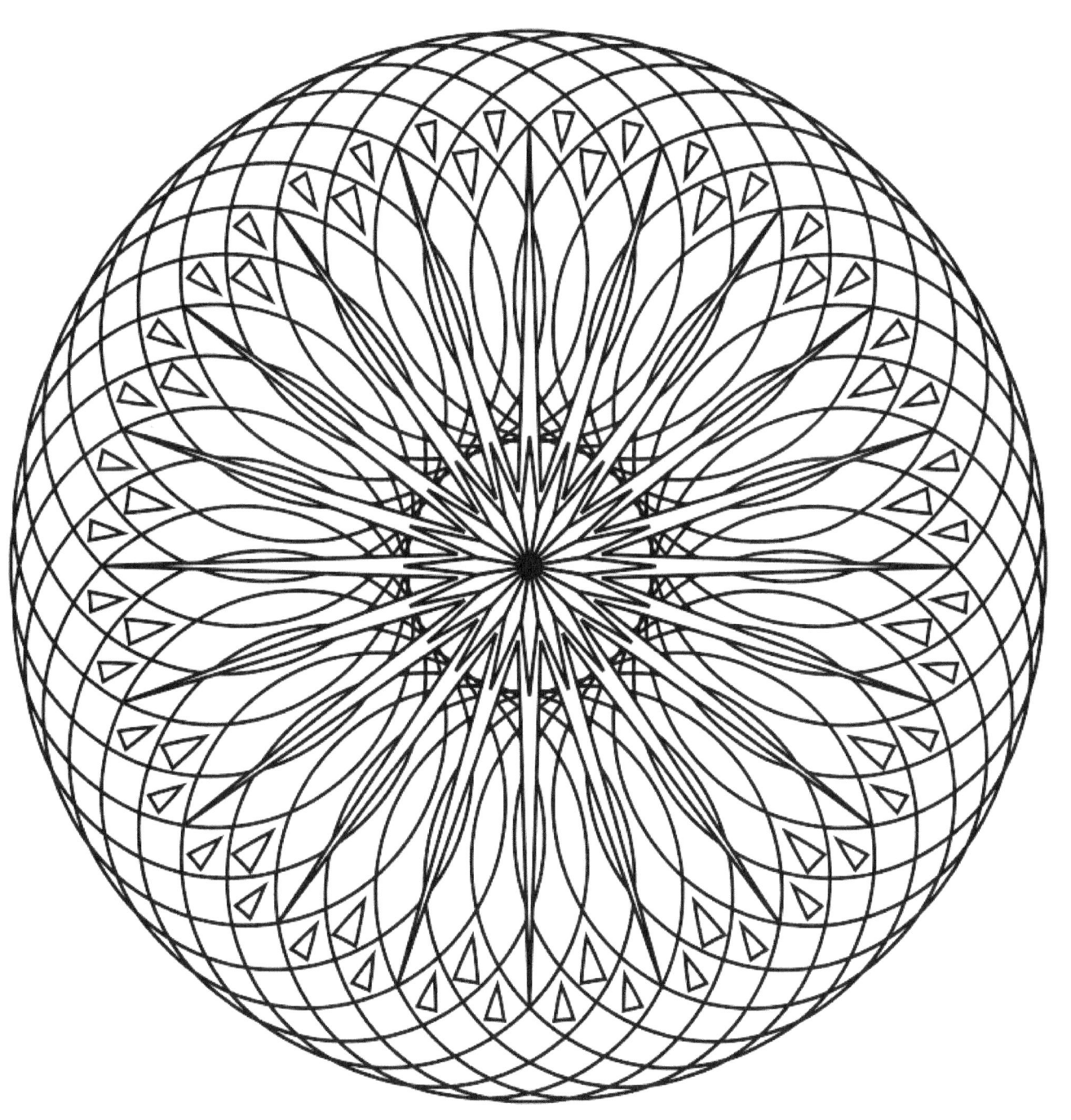

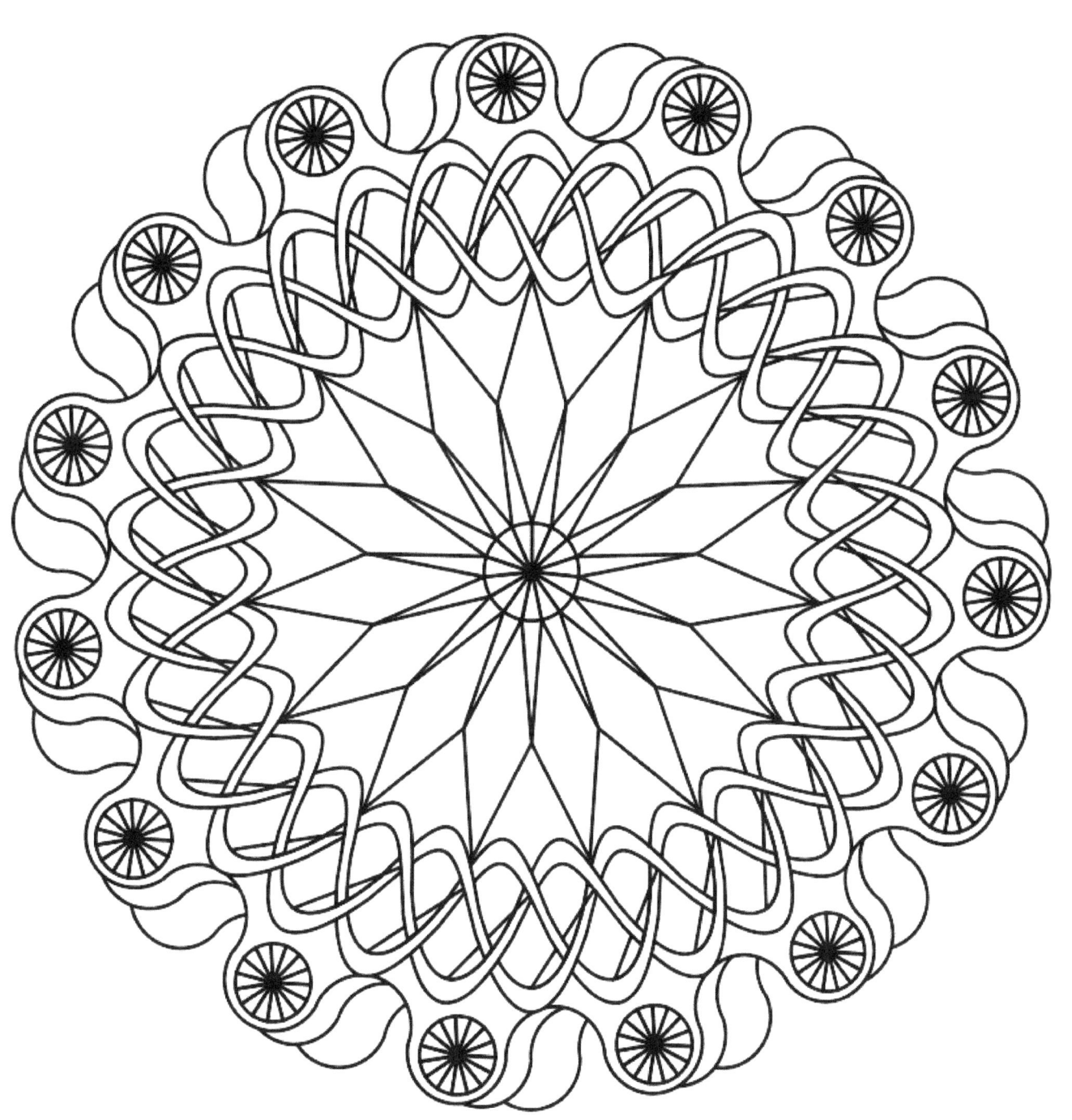

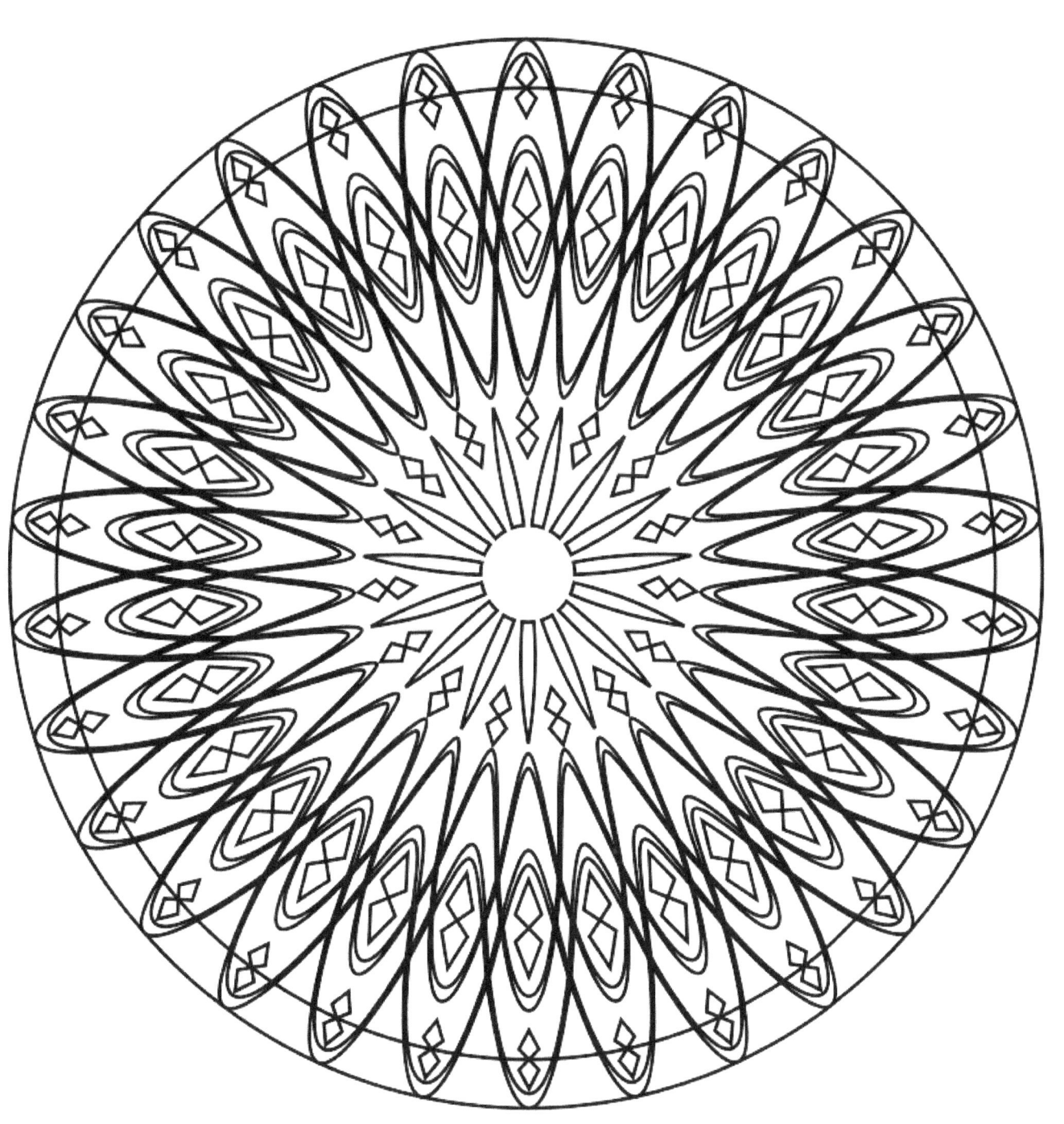

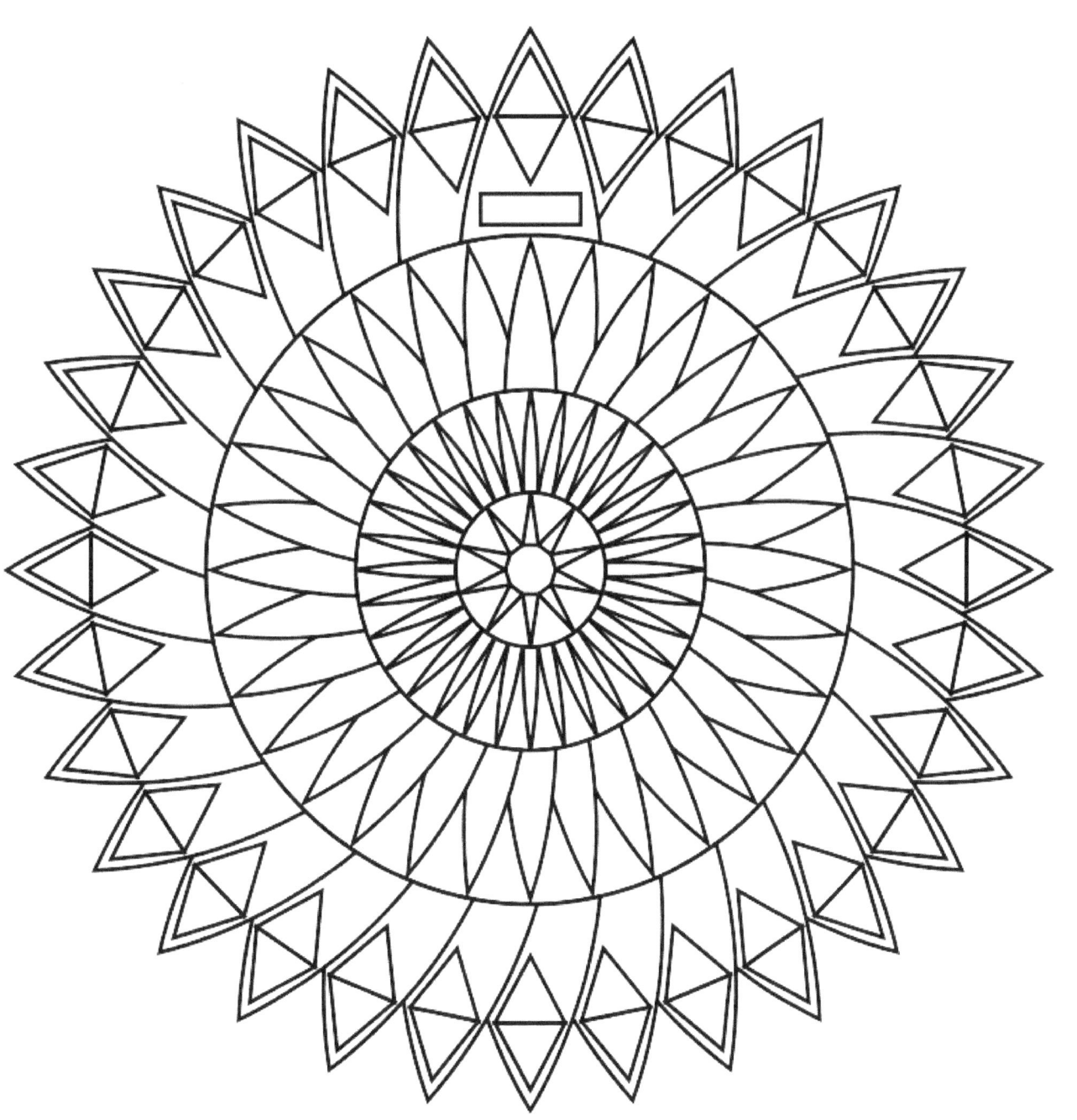

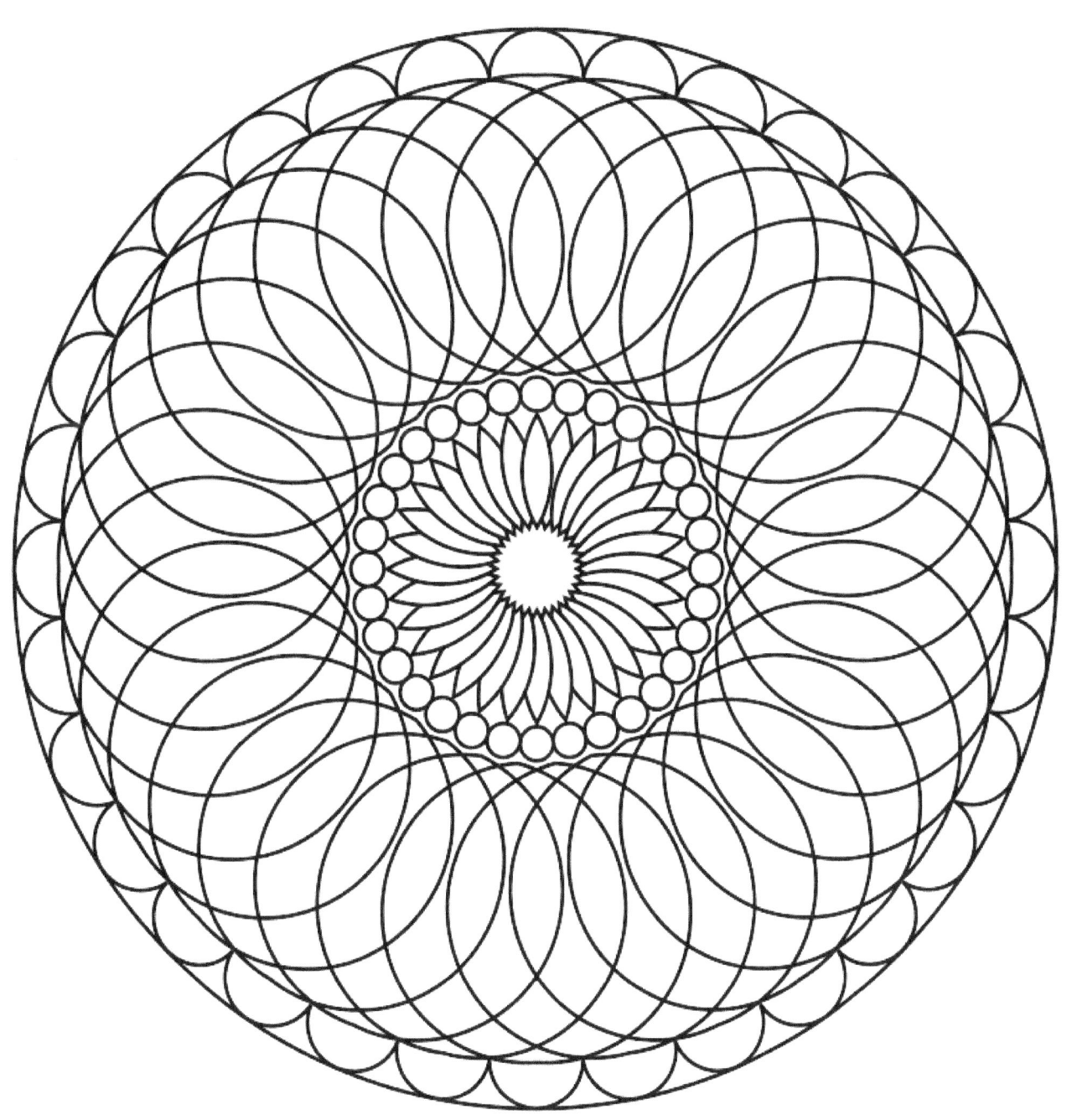

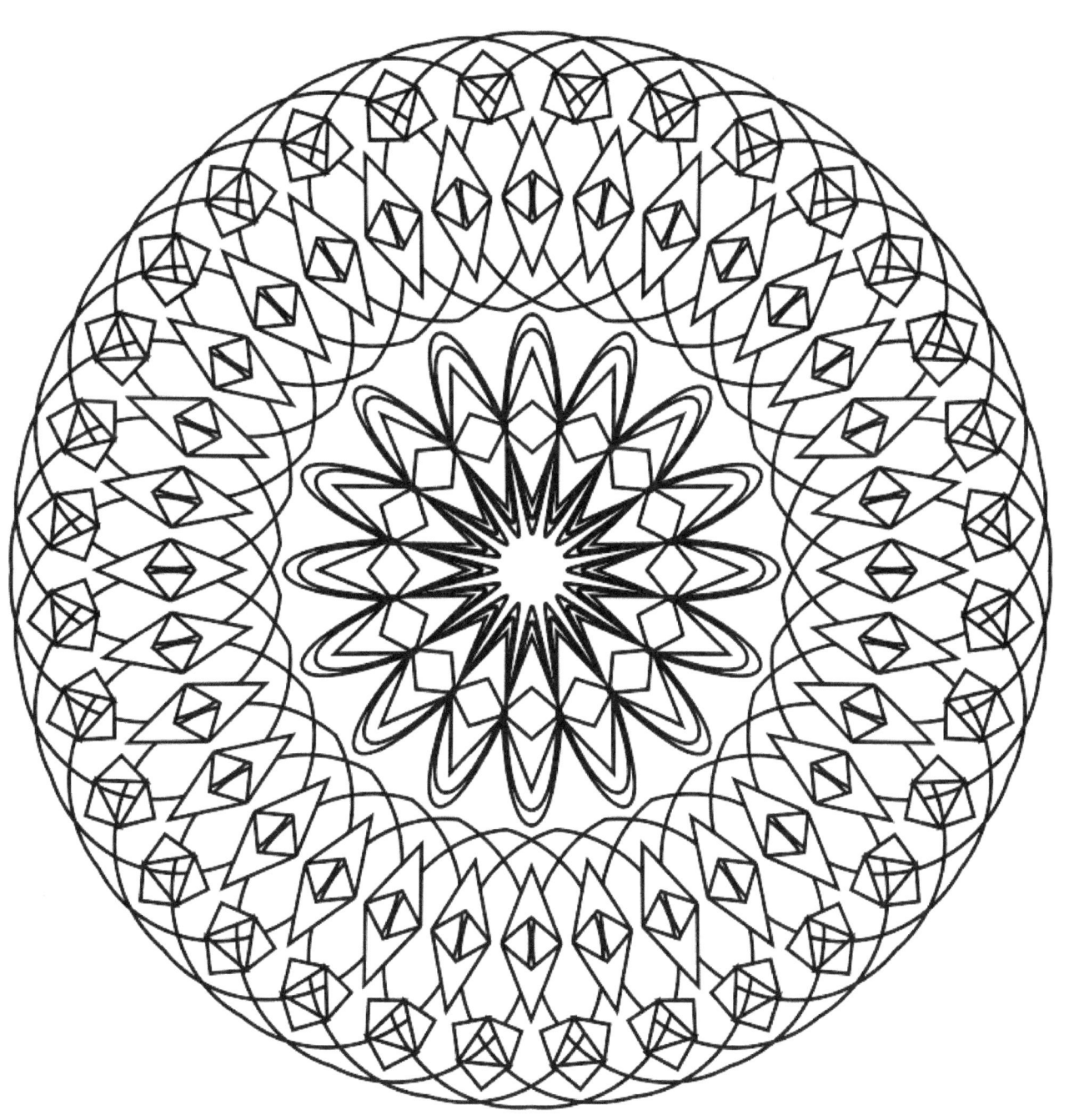

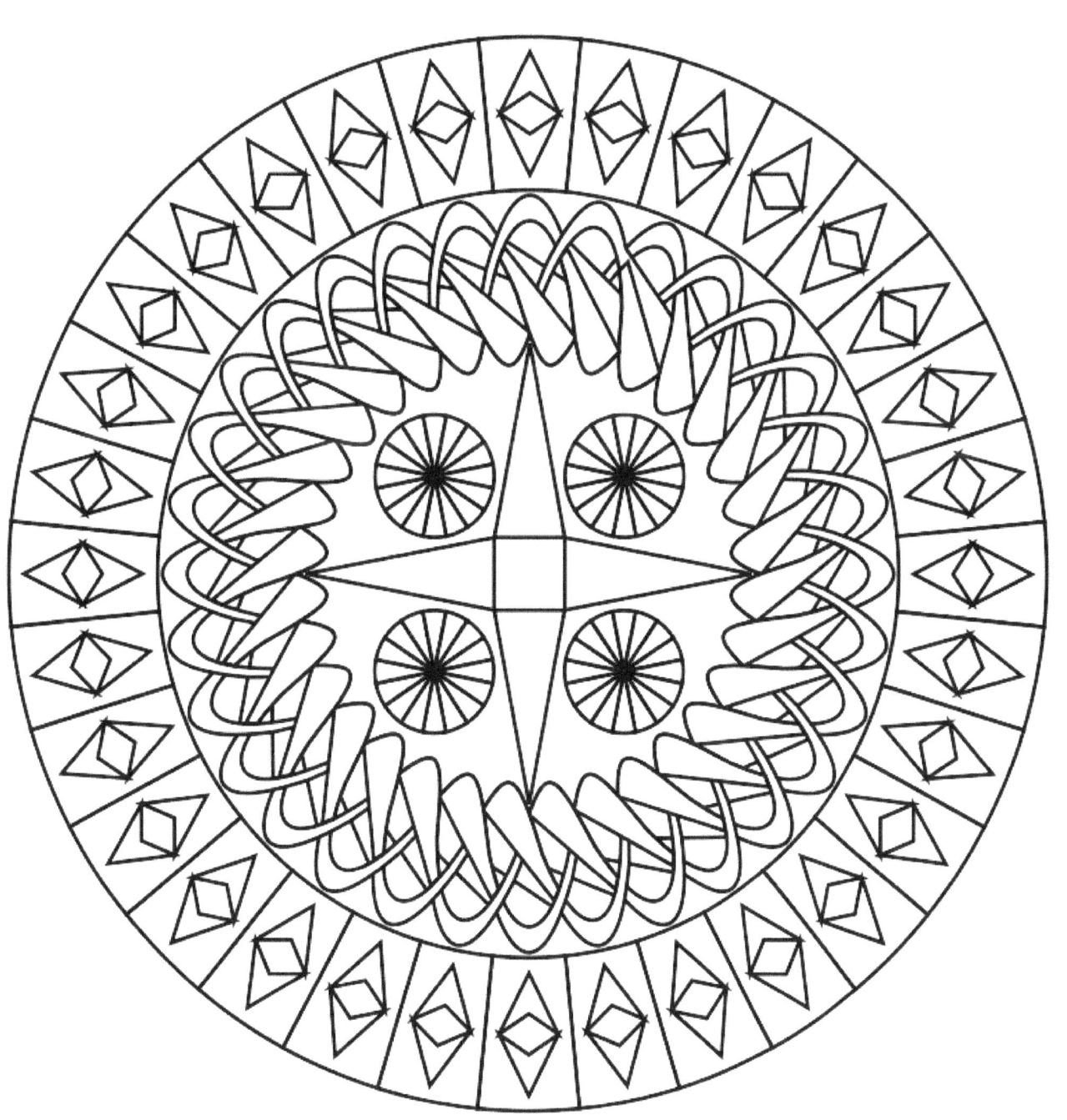

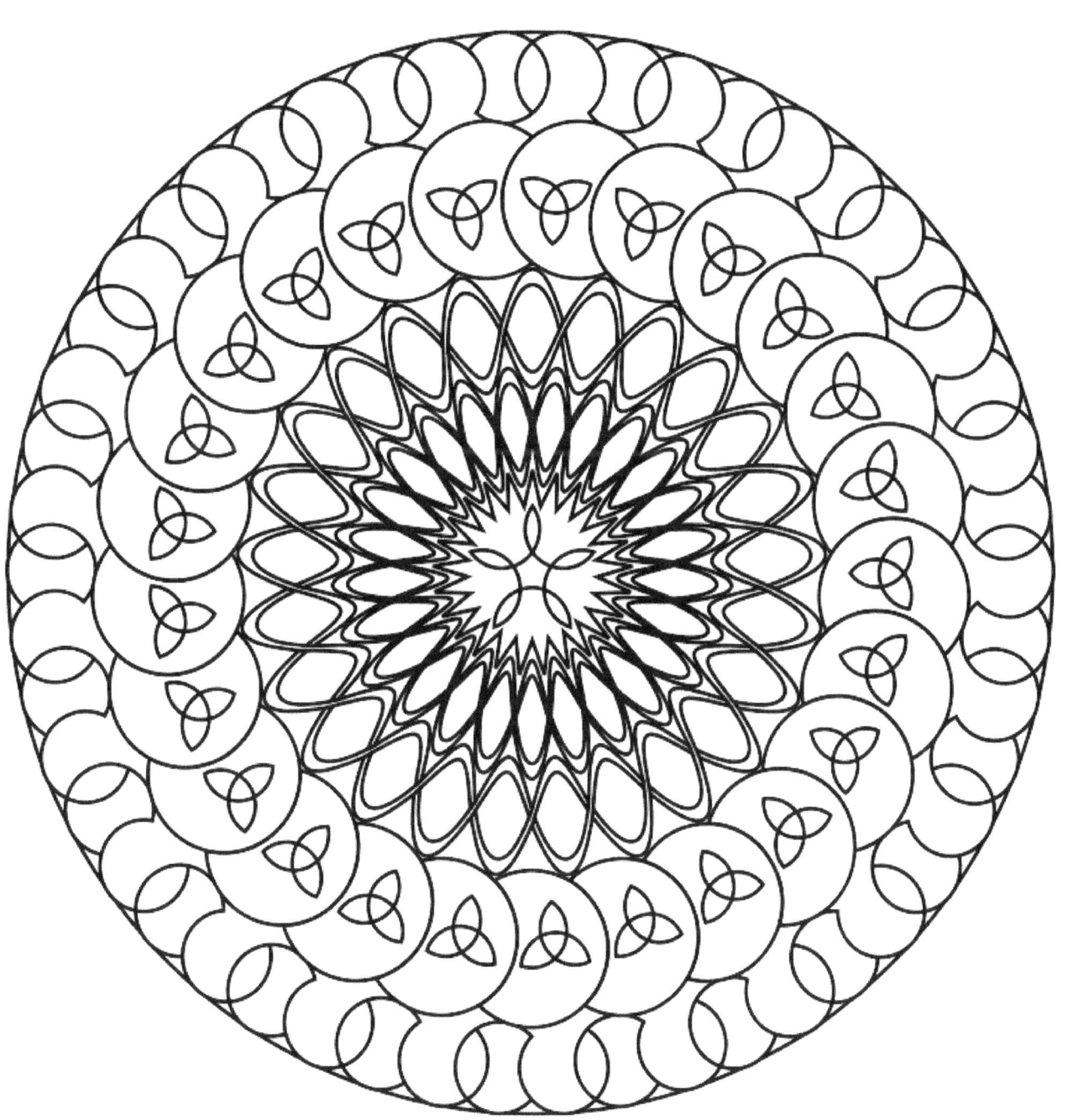

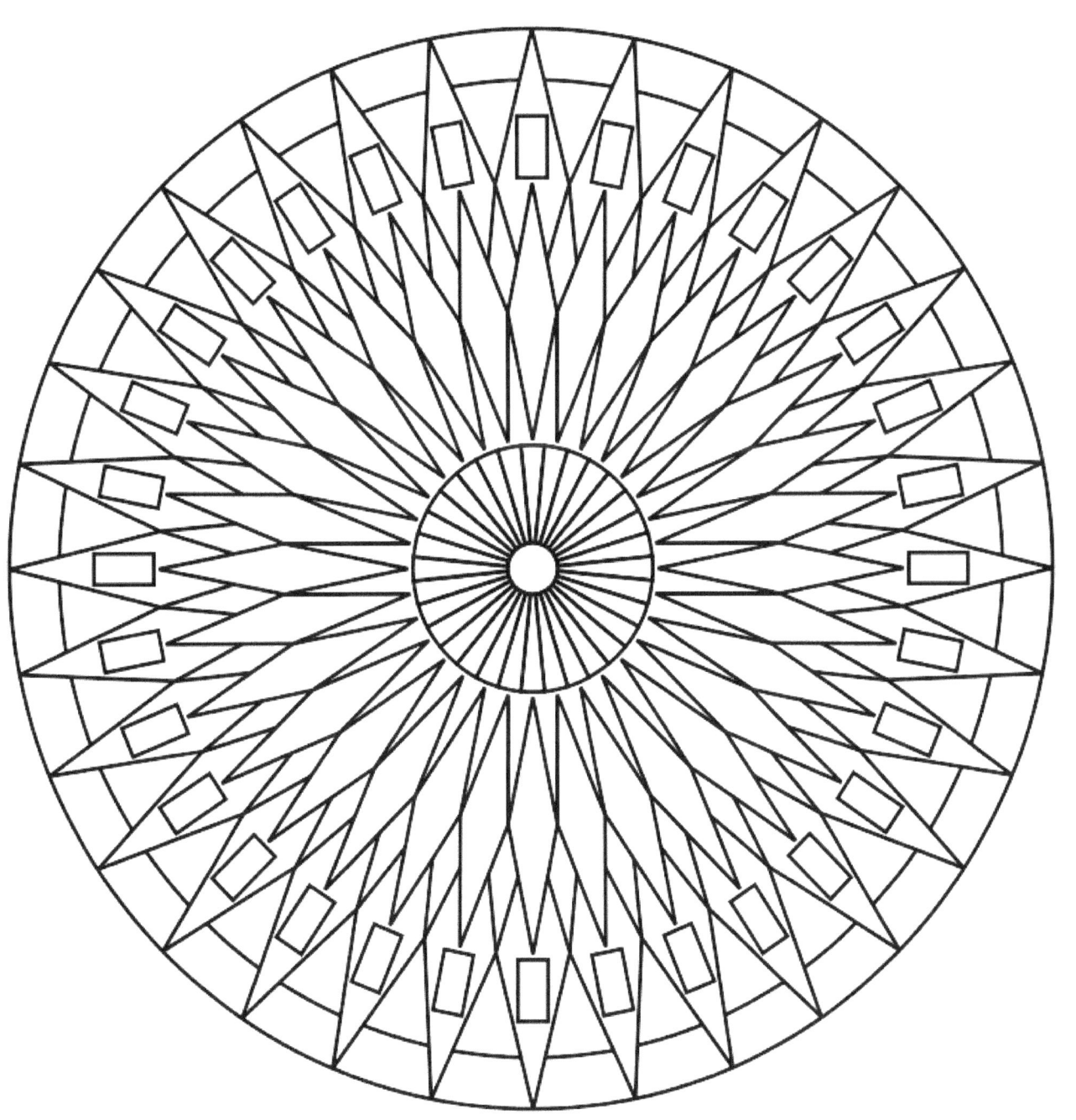

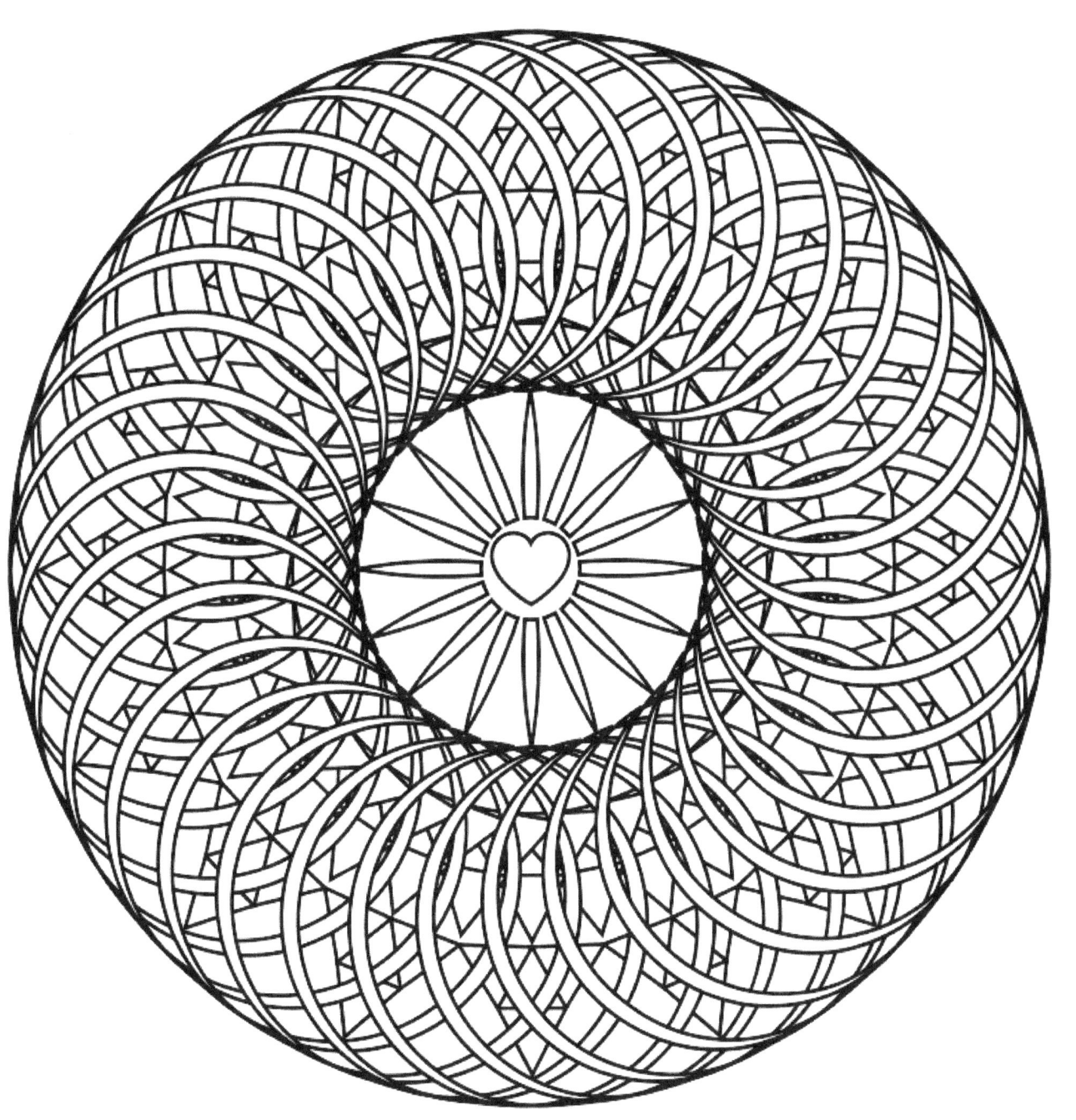

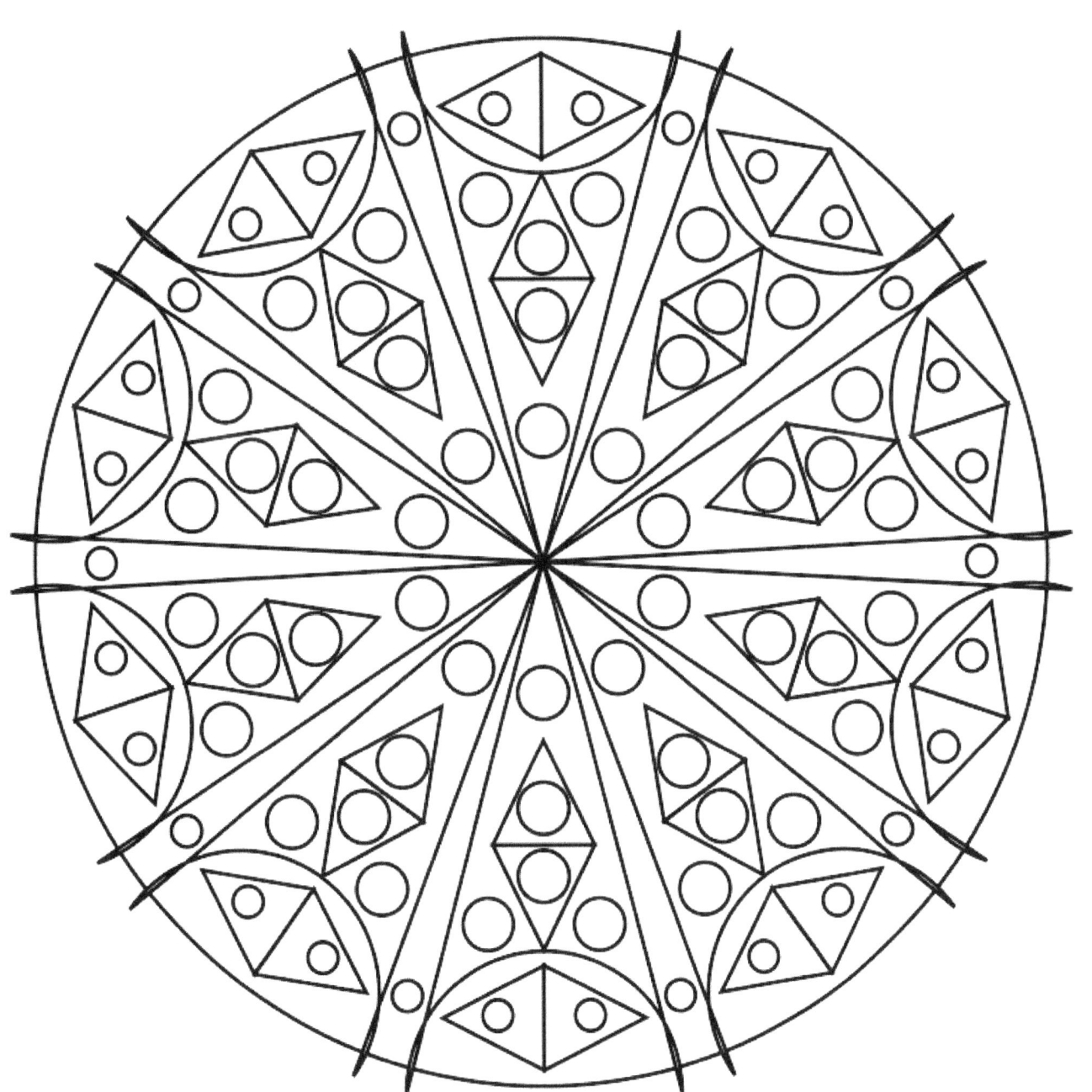

Final Words

If you enjoy my work, please feel free to join my mailing list at:
http://RomeoRocha.com

You can also follow me on Twitter at:
https://twitter.com/FRRMarketingLLC

You can Like my page on Facebook at:
https://facebook.com/AdultColoringBooksbyRo/

Thank you and happy coloring!!

www.ingramcontent.com/pod-product-compliance
Lightning Source LLC
Chambersburg PA
CBHW060010210526
45170CB00017B/2144